Although he's been out for quite a while, Brent Bill still remembers that high school can be both funny and frightening. In **Lunch Is My Favorite Subject,** he shows you how to get through the rigors and routines of high school with a sense of humor and reliance on God. This book provides a refreshing perspective on such intimidating subjects as English III, Driver Education, SAT/PSAT Skills Review, Spanish 1-2, Physical Science, Comparative Government, Geometry, and more. Whether you're a freshman, senior, between, or beyond, you're sure to enjoy **Lunch Is My Favorite Subject.**

BY J. Brent Bill

Rock and Roll
Stay Tuned
Lunch Is My Favorite Subject

LUNCH

Is My Favorite Subject

J. Brent Bill

Fleming H. Revell Company
Old Tappan, New Jersey

The Scripture quotation identified PHILLIPS is from THE NEW TESTA-
MENT IN MODERN ENGLISH, Revised Edition—J. B. Phillips, trans-
lator. © J. B. Phillips 1958, 1960, 1972. Used by permission of the
Macmillan Publishing Co., Inc.

Illustrations by Rob Suggs

Library of Congress Cataloging in Publication Data

Bill, J. Brent, 1951–
  Lunch is my favorite subject.

  Summary: Discusses various aspects of the high school experience grade by grade and how to cope by relying on one's
Christian faith.
  1. High school students—Conduct of life. [1. Conduct of
life. 2. Christian life. 3. High schools. 4. Schools] I. Title.
BJ1661.B48 1987   248.8′3   86-31312
ISBN 0-8007-5239-2

Copyright © 1987 by J. Brent Bill
Published by the Fleming H. Revell Company
Old Tappan, New Jersey 07675
Printed in the United States of America

To my dad,
John H. Bill,
who never dreamed I'd graduate from high school,
let alone write a book.
I surprised us both,
didn't I?

• CONTENTS ••

Eleventh Grade

Twelfth Grade

• ACKNOWLEDGMENTS ••

Though I get to put my name on the cover of this book, many people helped me with it. Since I don't intend to share any of the royalties with them, the least I can do is offer this page of thanks.

First, I'm grateful to all the Young Life, United Methodist Youth, and Young Friends who have put up with me as their leader over the last fifteen years. You've helped keep me young and worn me out at the same time. Most of all you've kept me aware of how fun and scary it is to be a high schooler. I've really enjoyed our times together and want you to know how much you mean to me.

Thanks also goes to the Guidance Department of Plainfield (Indiana) High School. Their student course-selection guide, *Pathfinder*, was the inspiration for many of the class descriptions that follow.

I owe a great debt of gratitude to my family—Sharon, Benjamin, and Timothy. They never knew what time supper was going to be, what time I'd get home at night, or if what I was writing was really going to be the million-seller I said it would be. Still they kept the faith and let me have my "writing nights." I *will* share the royalties with all of you.

Nancy Ragan, super secretary and faithful friend, endured this from the first draft to the last—and through it all gave me suggestions to make the book better. For all your effort and proofreading, Nancy, thanks. You're great, you know.

And finally, to all the rest of my family and friends whose names appear as teachers and students throughout the book. Now will you quit bugging me about putting *your* name in one of my books?

• INTRODUCTION ••

This is a book for teenagers by a teenager. All right, a former teenager. Okay, so I haven't been a teenager for over fifteen years. I still look like I did when I was seventeen. Well, I look a *little* bit like I did as a teen. To be truthful, the only way I look like I did as a teenager is that I am still a male. Instead of short and skinny with way too much hair, I now am short and chubby with way too little hair. Back then I dreamt of facial hair—having a mustache or beard seemed really manly. Now I've got it, but it's about the only hair I do have. I did get rid of the awful-looking, heavy black-framed glasses I used to avoid wearing. Now I've got contact lenses. So I don't look anything like I did then. I don't feel any older, though, except after a few hours of flag football or shooting hoops. It seems like I was a teenager just yesterday instead of over a decade ago. That's because my high school days were some of the best (and worst) years I've ever lived through. I couldn't, and wouldn't, ever want to forget them.

My most vivid memory of getting ready to go to high school is my father telling me to enjoy the next four years (he prayed nightly that I would get out after only four—and with my grades he had good reason to pray) because they would be the easiest and happiest of my life. After high school I would be an adult. And that was no fun. By the third day of my freshman year, I was sure he had been telling me a fairy tale. Like Santa Claus or the Easter Bunny—it just wasn't true. If this was the happiest time of my life, I wasn't sure I wanted to live through the rest of it.

Some kids find being a teenager neat. It *is* the best time of their lives. They are part of the crowd everyone wants to be a part of. They don't have terminal zits. They are good-looking and so are all of their friends. They have nice cars. They're athletically and scholastically gifted. They like everyone and everyone likes them—even their parents. But for some others, it's not so hot. They aren't part of any group, let alone the

11

right one. They may be in special classes. People talk about them, not because they like them, but because they like to make fun of them—even their parents.

For the rest of us it's a mixture. It's good and bad. Sometimes high school is a place where we belong, where we've got friends. It can also be a scary time, when we wonder if our friends really do like us or if they are hanging around because it's National Be Kind to a Nerd Week. One day we get along just fine with our folks, the next World War III has broken out at home and bodies litter the family room. We get an A in Spanish and a D in Algebra. We make the basketball team and then miss the free throw that would have made us the hero and our team city champs. Some days go by so fast they look like pages falling off a calendar in a 1930s movie. At other times the minutes in class seem to have been sucked into the "Twilight Zone," turning into decades.

The time that's supposed to be the best of our lives includes struggling desperately to understand all the crazy symbols of algebra and geometry and getting a C for our efforts. It is a time of being all too aware of how skinny (or fat or short or tall or whatever) we are. We know we don't fit in with the crowd we want to fit in with and are not too sure at times if we like being in the one we're in. We tell jokes that we think are a scream only to have our friends stare at us in horror that we would let anything so awful pass our lips. We go on dates with people we desperately want to fall in love with us, then squirt the mustard at McDonald's all over our Levis and dump our date's Cherry Coke on them as we scramble for napkins to clean ourselves up with.

Times change. So do fashions, music, movies, TV shows, and most everything else. Feelings don't. I wanted to be good-looking, smart, athletic, and "with it" when I was in high school. I wasn't any of those things. And no matter how hard I tried, wishing wouldn't make it so.

Chances are you're a lot like I was—just an average kid. Not too cool but not too nerdy. That's okay. Because I found out that I wasn't an average kid. And you aren't either. There's no such thing. We all have gifts and talents that make us unique. There's no one just like you anywhere. Before you clap your hands and sarcastically thank heaven, stop. You are here for a reason. That's important. You may not know what that reason is yet, but there is one. You're a special person that God wants the best, not worst, to happen to. Surviving this time of your life is a lot easier when you take time to include God in it.

Your years in high school can be some of the best years of your life. Though at times it will seem like life is crashing in and you will positively die from the sheer living of it, you won't. Things that scare the socks off you now, will be remembered later with great fits of laughter.

Right now, of course, the important thing is surviving it so you *can* laugh about it later. That's what this book is about. We'll spend the next few pages going through high school—looking at the funny and scary parts, and how your faith fits in. I hope you'll learn more than how to survive it. I hope you'll learn how to enjoy it—even the bad times. So sit back and relax. Let's take a walk through life at Mullenville High School—home of the "Fightin' Warthogs." Hey, I think I hear the school bell now.

LUNCH

Is My Favorite Subject

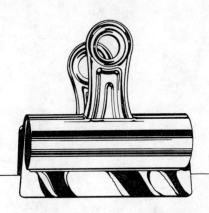

MULLENVILLE SCHOOL DISTRICT
Official Class Schedule

Thomas	John	Alan	9	118
(last)	(first)	(middle)	(grade)	(homeroom)
123 Pleasant Valley Lane		Mullenville	555-5555	437
(street)		(city)	(phone)	(locker)

Class	Code	Room	Mon.	Tues.	Wed.	Thurs.	Fri.
English 9	e–010	212	X	X	X	X	X
Algebra 1–2	m–312	309	X	X	X	X	X
Phys Ed	p–851	gym	a–314	X	a–314	X	a–314
Biology	s–416	112	X	X	X	X	X
Lunch		caf					
State His	h–201	115	X	X	X	X	X
Exp Art	a–480	316	X	s–112	X	s–112	
Study Hall		in main auditorium					
Spanish 1–2	f–150	217	X	X	X	X	X

Note: Numbers appearing in weekly schedule indicate study hall seat assignments.

• THE FIRST DAY OF HIGH SCHOOL ••

Coming soon, to a neighborhood near you, the terrifying tale of one of adolescence's most horrific moments. You may have been scared silly seeing *Friday the 13th*, parts 1–26, hollered yourself hoarse at *Hallowe'en 12*, but you've experienced nothing like the horror of

The First Day of High School.

Until you experience it you really don't know what fear means. See kids you know and look up to wander aimlessly like zombies through strange buildings. See teachers, who appear almost human, hand out seven hours of homework per class per night. Hear your own voice suddenly asking incredibly stupid-sounding questions and telling jokes that aren't close to being funny. Watch your up-till-then-clear complexion turn into something that resembles a supreme pizza—just minutes before your big date. Yes, you'll want to run home and hide long before *The First Day of High School* is over. There's no escaping it though, it will get you soon. Beware of

The First Day of High School.

• • • •

My first day of high school is one day I'll never forget—no matter how hard I try. It was the first Tuesday after Labor Day 1966. That's a long time ago, I know. You probably weren't even born yet. But read on and you'll discover that some things never change.

My best friend, Greg, and I had finally made the move from Hilltonia Junior High School and were headed for the big time—Columbus West High School. West was the only high school on our side of town. Built in the twenties in a sort of neoclassic institutional style, it was the center of all that was cool on "The Hilltop." Being there would bring us one giant step closer to adulthood. All our older friends were there. Even Mom and Dad and my aunts and uncles had gone there. At long last it was my turn to enter those hallowed halls and bring scholastic honor to the family name. How was I to know what lay in wait for me behind the scarred, green-painted front doors of the main lobby?

It was a bright, sunny day. The air was a little cool for early September, but not so cool that I'd have to ruin my specially picked out clothing ensemble by wearing a stupid jacket. I got up early because I was too excited to sleep. After all, if I was going to start high school then my driver's license couldn't be too far off. Plus, now that I was a high schooler, and not a wimpy little junior higher, it was okay to drool over members of the opposite sex, instead of going "Ugh!" Then would come college, then my own apartment—away from my folks. My parents were okay as far as parents go, but they were still parents.

I dressed in my best Levis, button-down shirt, and Converse tennis shoes (black with purple laces—definitely cool) and headed out the door. Greg, who wasn't nearly as cool as I was, but still a long way from nerd, met me at the corner and we were on our way. We had a mile and half hike to "Waste High." We were heady with the anticipation of how happy the upperclassmen would be to see us finally gracing the school with our presence. We were, after all, two of the coolest, funniest, and best-looking underclassmen to ever appear. We were so cool that we kicked things out of our way as we walked down the side streets, heading ever West-ward. Then came the Beer Can. Greg and I spotted it at the same time and took off running to see who could get to it first and send it into orbit. He won. He aimed. He kicked. He shouldn't have. It was full. It was also open. I laughed, but not so long that he would get mad and pound me. His clothes reeked of Eau de Miller High Life. To prove he was a good sport about going to school smelling like one of the Anhueser-Busch kids, he picked up the can and poured what was left of it on me.

It was an omen of how the rest of the day would go.

No one told us how big the place was. Sure we'd been driven by the place before, but things are a lot bigger in person than when you're zooming by in a car. The pillars lining the front doors looked as if they had been hewn from giant California Redwoods and probably had blinking red lights on top to warn low-flying 707s. And there were all those kids. I was sure Mr. Randall, the principal, was on the phone to the school board telling them how they had made a mistake and sent every kid in Columbus to West. Surely the seven other high schools in town were empty, hungry for high schoolers. But no, all those kids, just like us, belonged there.

Not only did the seniors *not* have a party to welcome us there, they ignored us. They walked around us, scowling down from their average heights of ten feet four inches—and that was the girls. The upper-class guys lounged around, cracking jokes and swapping stories, as obviously in place as we were out. We looked up and down halls that seemed to have been designed as a set for a Vincent Price horror movie. Greg and I huddled close together for safety in this no-kid's-land that wasn't quite what we had expected. I think I heard Greg sobbing silently under his breath. Of course it could have been me.

A voice that made Darth Vader's sound sweeter than the Welcome Wagon lady's (it turned out to be Mr. Randall) called out over the antiquated P.A. system. We weren't sure what it said, something like "UNYJONNNHXDIHUH-DIHDHUYNEUC DHYJIUIYUH." Neither of us knew what that meant, but since everyone else who looked like a freshman (and they were easy to spot since they all had on new Levis, button-down shirts, and black Converse tennies) seemed to be moving toward the auditorium, Greg and I joined them. We found seats that were carved full of initials dating back to the twenties. Then out came Mr. Randall—all seventeen feet and fifteen hundred pounds of him. (Turned out that he was really only five nine, but he was standing on the stage that day and we *were* only freshmen.) His voice came out clearly this time, he didn't need a microphone to talk to a bunch of underclassmen. He began laying down the law. He told us what was expected from us and what better never come from us. He went on for twenty minutes, and every other word was *horseplay* or *shenanigans*. I gathered that he was against them. Everything he said could be reduced to what became known as Randall's rule: "If it's fun, forget it."

After the Big R left the stage, the registrar came out and

gave us our homeroom assignments and class schedules. That was okay, but what I really wanted was either a map of the place, marked by AAA with my class route, or a ride home. I didn't get either. Then the starting bell rang and we were off, turned loose to try and find our way to our first class. Within the three-minute time limit.

So it was out into the halls—those seemingly endless labyrinths—all filled with giants. Armed with only our coolness and wit—both of which seemed to have deserted us the minute we entered the building. Why had we forsaken the safety of junior high?

Sound anything like *your* first day? I'll bet it does. Obviously, I lived. Either that or some alien took over my body and has been living in it for the last seventeen years. (And made a real bad mistake picking this body out of all the billions of choices.) I did get lost a time or two (or three or four) during the first few days. I even sat through the wrong class once, just because I was too embarrassed to admit I was in the wrong place. Now I go back to West and the halls don't terrify me and the imposing columns are really only three stories high. Some things don't change, though—the seniors still look down on me.

Columbus West High School, home of the Cowboys, was only terrifying when it was unknown territory. As things became familiar so did it. It turned into a rather nice place to be—except for classes of course. All my friends spent their time the same place I did. My locker became my second home. A sort of gunmetal gray split-level, with books and school stuff on the top shelf and the important things like tennis rackets and *Mad* magazines down below. Even the creaky old building itself had some nifty things about it, like the courtyard in the middle. Even if we weren't allowed out into it. There was Magly Field, where the football team and I spent all my Friday nights. I wasn't on the team, but two thousand other kids and I were there every fall Friday evening. My life centered around West. I was a Cowboy. It was *my* turf.

That's an important thing to remember about being a high schooler. New things sometimes seem scary. Or they don't happen just the way you thought they would as you lie in bed dreaming about them. But that's okay. Even though things like the first day of high school can be scary, they can also be exciting.

That doesn't mean they will be less scary. My first day of school wasn't fun, but it was exciting. It was like the first time I ever went skiing. I put on the skis confident that I would schuss like Jean-Claude Killy. Instead I zoomed uncontrollably down the slopes on my tush, like Jean-Clod Billy. Trees kept jumping in my way. So did other skiers. Forty-five falls and thirty minutes later I reached the bottom. I had been scared (and treed) almost to death—but I sure was excited.

Excitement and fun are not always synonymous. But the exciting things are what takes life out of the ordinary into the special. They make life worth living.

You need to learn to savor unexpected and unfamiliar things instead of fearing them.

Look at the disciples. Before they met Jesus they lived nice ordinary lives. They got up, ate breakfast, went to work, came home, ate supper, visited with the family, then went to bed. Then came Jesus. He called them out of ordinary to excitement. Their lives were forever changed. They went places they'd never even dreamed of. They worked miracles. They were hunted by the authorities. Later, most of them died martyrs' deaths. They were never the same again after their time with Jesus. They went out to change the world. They took to the seas, going places that just a while before they had never heard of. I doubt Peter, James, and John would say their lives with Jesus were fun. Exciting? Yes. Jesus energized their normal, boring lives.

Jesus is the same today. We need to let Him be a part of the first day of high school and every other day, too. That's not to say He'll make them all fun and games. He won't. High school life also won't always be just the way we want it. We may not get the date with the guy or girl we want. We may flunk a big test. But if we have the Lord of excitement with us, we can go places boldly instead of fearfully.

If Jesus is with us, the first day of high school can be a thrill instead of a chill.

Mrs. Benjamin: JoAnn, I have a question. Just what is this list you've given me?

JoAnn: It's just where I want my phone, TV, stereo . . .

Mrs. Benjamin: So, why are you telling me?

JoAnn: Well, this is *home*room, isn't it?

• • • •

Homeroom. Ever wonder why it's called that? It can't be because it's like any room at home. It isn't. Most of our houses don't have rooms with chalkboards on three walls and a bulletin board on the other. I don't know of any with forty-three desks and chairs in them either. And there aren't too many painted in that awful industrial green or beige. But you go to school and they put you in something called a homeroom. When you think about it, it raises a lot of questions. Is the homeroom teacher your new mommy or daddy? Do you ask them for lunch money or permission to go on a date on a school night? While you like large families, did you suddenly acquire forty-two new brothers and sisters? Do you have to treat them like real brothers and sisters or can you treat them like humans? And then comes the big one—do you have to buy them each a Christmas present?

At times like this I think high school raises more questions than it answers.

Regardless of all the questions, here you are—in homeroom with all these other kids, whom you may or may not see the rest of the day. Every weekday morning, regardless of what else is going on, you will march in, sit down with your new family, and begin your day.

I suppose homeroom is meant to be a sort of home base—a place of familiar faces. We all know it's a place the administration came up with so they could find out who's there and who's not so they can send the school S.W.A.T. team after the not theres. In spite of that, the thought of having a home base to start from each day is nice. You get together with others who are fighting the same fight you are—to someday actually graduate from the place and win your freedom. It's there you find out whether Marvin's making it through math or Buffy's blowing basketweaving. In homeroom you can also get advice on overcoming your latest Social Studies dilemma. Some of it may even be helpful. You find out whose taking who (or not taking who, so you can ask them yourself) to the homecoming dance. Homeroom can be a lot like home.

Homeroom can also be like church. Or maybe church should be like homeroom. Church should be a place where you go to get yourself energized and organized before you begin a new week. It should be a place to find out how others of God's family are doing—or not doing. You go there to learn some new "survival skills" for people of faith in enemy territory. It is there you get strength for facing life's challenges.

Church, like homeroom, can be a chance to catch up on what's going on in others' lives. Not to be gossipy, but because you care. Knowing that everyone else is facing the same joys and sorrows you are can help you feel a part of one another. It can give you an opportunity to help someone out, sometimes with something a lot more important than a geometry problem. It can also be a place where you find someone who can help you.

In the singing, Scripture reading, prayers, and preaching you can find the answers to life's questions. You can talk to the God who cares for you like a member of the family. Because you are.

When you drag your weary body to homeroom, dreading another exciting day at Millard Fillmore Memorial High School, remember the last time you did the same at First Church. Could there be a need for a slight attitude adjustment? Maybe you need to see church as the homeroom of your life, a place that will even help you cope with homeroom at school.

Church and homeroom have one other thing in common: They are both what you make of them. If they are boring and a waste, it may be because you haven't made much of an effort to make them otherwise. You usually get out of something just about what you put into it. Like it says on some pop bottles, "No deposit, no return." If you don't put something into church or homeroom, you won't get much out. Think about it. You need to invest yourself to get a worthwhile return.

Homeroom and church. Church and homeroom. Both can be a home base from which to fight the good fights of school and life. As you sit in homeroom, looking at the day ahead, seeing your friends' bodies tense with anticipation of the first class, think of your spiritual homeroom—the church.

(e-010)

This course is designed for the student with an average-to-good command of basic language skills and will be taken by most students. The student will work in the Writer's Gallery on an individualized program in grammar and writing and will also spend time on fiction, speech, and language skills.

• • • •

Mrs. Sudsberry: Okay, today we're going to talk about grammar. Who would like to say something about grammar? How about you, Steve?
Steve: Whose?
Mrs. Sudsberry: Whose what?
Steve: Whose grammar?
Mrs. Sudsberry: Why ours, of course.
Steve: I can't do that, we're not even related. How am I supposed to talk about our Gramma?
Mrs. Sudsberry (somewhat frustrated): How about someone else? Yes, Ryan . . .
Ryan: My Grammar lives in a nice old house on Oak Street just across from Mrs. Miller.

• • • •

Don't you just love course descriptions like the one above? They're so hard to figure out. What is a Writer's Gallery—a place where the teachers get to take up BB guns and shoot at you if you get a bad grade on a paper? That's what it sounds like.

Okay, Whitney, you got a *D* on this composition. Up to the Writer's Gallery right now and strap yourself into the seat. Mr. Tridle, get your gun ready. Every time Whitney comes across the target area you may shoot. If you miss her she gets to write another paper. But every hit is a letter grade off her paper. Just put a quarter in the slot and press start when you're ready.

Speech?! We've been speaking since we were two years old. Some of us were even understandable then. Of coure, there are some people who are ninety-nine and can't be understood. Like our parents. Okay, so maybe instruction in speech is necessary.

What about language skills? Are they like gymnastics skills? If you learn them, are you going to be able to do fancy things with words? Have them use parallel bars or something? It's only after you've worked on language skills that you learn it's about how to use words better than you could before. But if the description said "learning how to use words better then you could before" it wouldn't sound as exotic and challenging as "language skills."

Then there's fiction. Don't worry too much about it. You'll only get a taste of it in English 9. Most of it comes in English 11 and 12. Try not to get too excited.

English 9 can be intimidating (if you don't know what that means, look it up in a dictionary, it's under *scary*), and not just because of the course descriptions. As you progress in school you'll learn that course descriptions are a lot like one of the subjects you'll study in English 9—fiction. That is, they more closely resemble a figment of the English department's imagination than they do real life. So set the course description aside and don't fret. What's *really* scary are all the rules about using English.

By now you've been hearing words come out of your mouth for about thirteen years. Some of your parents would swear you were talking the day you were born—and haven't shut up since. You've been writing words since you were six or seven. You know what subjects, verbs, adverbs, and adjectives are and how to use them. Now some teacher gives you a book that's about three-miles thick, full of all kinds of legislation regarding these words you've been using all of your life. You've got to deal with possessive singular nouns, conjunctions introducing independent clauses ("Hello Santa, let me introduce you to Ms. Claus"), future perfect progressive, gerunds, and all kinds of other things.

The good news is you've probably been doing all this and

just didn't know it. You had the ability but didn't know what to call all this grammatical mumbo jumbo. The bad news is, now you've got to. If you don't, you'll not only bring disgrace to the English-speaking people of the world (all 800 million or so of us, I know *I'll* be upset) but you'll also get an *F*. You decide which is worse.

For all its frustrations though, English 9 can be rewarding. Now you're not just dependent on the language you got secondhand from parents and others, it's your own. You know the rules and regulations and are acquiring the skills that enable you to make the words do what you want. You can make them go through hoops and paint pretty pictures for the mind's eye. You can even bend the rules to make your words do more powerful things. *Sentence fragments.* They're really powerful when you know what you're doing. If you don't. Not much good. Are. They?

English rules are guides to good communication. God's rules are guides to good living. Just as grammar helps us use our language most effectively, God's guides help us live our lives to the fullest. English 9 shows that rules don't really restrain us, but set us free to use words to their fullest potential.

That's how it is with God's laws. They may seem exacting. Some of them we even wonder about. But they are there for our own good. They benefit us as we learn to live by them. They are there to keep us from falling into traps—emotional, physical, and otherwise—from which we might never escape. If we break a rule of grammar, the worst things that happen are that our friends don't understand what we are trying to say or we get an *F* in class. Breaking God's rules can mess our lives up.

So, try to remember this parallel between grammar and God. You might even want to offer a word or sentence or even a paper of thanks. Then maybe you'll not only write good, you'll also live good. *Well,* I mean.

This course is designed for the freshman math student who has a stronger math background than is required for General Math. Topics to be studied are: real number systems, sets, inequalities, equations, graphs, polynomials, functions, etc. This course develops the student's ability to think in a more abstract way and prepares him or her for Geometry and Algebra 3-4.

• • • •

Mrs. Kramer: Lisa, would you please come up and give us the answer to the following equation $E = \dfrac{Ff(\quad); X}{(P-X)\, p}$

Lisa: ???

Mrs. Kramer: Do we have a problem there, Lisa?

Lisa: Yes, there are two problems. The first is the one on the board and the second is I don't know the answer.

• • • •

Mathematics are difficult. But then, I'm not telling you anything you don't already know, am I? Everyone knows that math is hard. Except me. I didn't. When I signed up for algebra, I was excited and ready to take it on. I wish someone would have at least warned me. I had done okay at arithmetic—gotten As and Bs in long division even. I thought to myself, *How hard can math be?* I found out.

I had a rather romantic notion of what algebra was all about. My first encounter with it was on the old "Ozzie and Harriet" show on TV (some of you may know about it from late-night reruns). Ozzie and Harriet Nelson's kids, Ricky (the rock and roll star) and David, were shown doing algebra in one episode. I was mesmerized. I don't remember the show's plot at all, but all the Xs and Ys and ( )s looked like lots of fun. From that moment on I could hardly wait to get to ninth grade and start on the good stuff. Good-bye baby arithmetic—hello major math.

I should have stayed in the minors. Algebra 1-2 was the beginning of three nightmare years of mathematics. The Xs and Ys and other things that were supposed to be transformed into numbers never were. Algebra was like a secret code created by the KGB. How as I, a mere freshman, supposed to crack it? Sure, most of the other kids did. But they were probably agents planted by the Kremlin. The teacher definitely was on the other side. It didn't take a CIA agent to figure that out. The other kids got As and Bs while I got Ds.

I realize now that I was not one of the kids referred to in the course description. In fact I may not have been able to master General Math. I'm not sure, even with all my advanced wisdom and years, I could get it now.

Some people are mathematical geniuses. Not me. Even when I thought I got it, I didn't. I liked math, but I didn't understand it. And for me, liking and understanding it were three different things.

I envied those who got it right off. I envied those who got it after lots of hard work. I even envied those who got it but didn't understand *how* they got it. I didn't come close to any of those.

You may be like me—struggling with every equation. Or you may be one of those who looks at it and understands it immediately. Either way, it's okay. Because either way you can see how important it is. It has value—a lot of value. Mathematics are all around us. People use math all the time. I just wish I understood it better.

There is one thing even those of us who cannot understand it can come to appreciate about math—that's the order and rightness of it. In a mathematics problem there is only one right answer. (That's what made it hard for me, sometimes I had one that was close, but close didn't count.) If you follow the laws and principles governing math you will always solve the problem. You can count on that.

I'm glad God knows algebra. And all other kinds of math as well. Just imagine if He didn't. The planets on elliptical orbits would be crashing into those on circular ones. Stars would career all over the place. Everything in the universe would go bouncing into every other thing, making a general mess—especially of us people who lived on one planet that happened to run into another. Something like that could ruin your whole day.

The orderliness of God is impressive. The solar system runs right. Earth spins as it should so that our lives are possible. We don't have to lie awake nights worrying that Mercury is going to crash through the wall into our bedroom (if it does, it's probably Aunt Martha's 1975 Comet with 12,623 miles on it—she didn't do too well at math either and so missed the curve outside the house).

The things God put into place stay there. To borrow from a restaurant commercial, God does it right, or He doesn't do it.

So while you're trying to figure out why X, Y, and Z just don't get out of math and back to the alphabet where they belong, remember God, the great mathematician. Be thankful that the One who put it all together knew how to keep it all together. And if you are really struggling, you may even want to ask for a little help with the problem you've just copied off the blackboard.

• PHYSICAL EDUCATION ••

The required physical education course includes units in football, speedball, handball, gymnastics, dance, basketball, softball, swimming, wrestling, track, and fitness. Grades are determined by a balance of competence, correct dress for class, and participation.

• • • •

Mr. Buck: Okay, class, here's what we're going to do today. I want you all to line up against the wall over there. Hulk, you come here. Here's this half-inflated all-purpose ball. Now we're going to play a little dodge ball. You guys against the wall—the object of the game is to not let Hulk hit you with the ball, thereby surviving to go on to your next class. Any questions? . . . Sorry, I don't have time to answer them.
Let the games begin.
Class: Our Father, which art in heaven. . . .

• • • •

Physical education. There's nothing like it. It refreshes the soul. Improves the body. And teaches you how to lie so still that Hulk will think you're really dead and won't hit you with that rubber ball. Because if he does, you won't have to play dead, you'll *be* dead.

I confess I don't know much about girls' phys ed classes—though after my first round of dodge ball I did try to get into one. I do know that guys' phys ed makes Army survival week in basic training look like it was designed for wimps. Dodge ball is just one example. Do you know of any other time when some stranger tells you to throw a half-inflated ball (it stings more that way) and try to maim your best friend? The killer look on the face of the kid who just led a peace march against nuclear war is really scary. And that ball leaves a red mark the size of New Jersey on your thigh when it hits you. That's if you're lucky enough to get hit on the thigh. But dodge ball is only one of the many exciting things you get to do in guys' phys ed. You also get to get spiked on the top of your head by volleyballs coming at 1,200 mph after being slammed by the eight-foot gorillas on the other team, have rope burns from climbing hand over hand to the gymnasium ceiling and sliding all the way down the rope because your arms gave out just before you reached safety, play friendly games of touch football that always turn into something resembling a gang war when the phys ed teacher goes to the equipment room, and much more. Instead of being issued gym shorts, tennis shoes, T-shirts, and sweats, you feel like you ought to be given a rifle and a helmet. It's frightening.

Phys ed is something we all get to experience, male and female alike. Even though we've been talking about guys' phys ed, there is something that they share. It's that the name of the class isn't quite right. It's only half right. It is *physical.* There is no doubt that you have to be physical just to survive. The education part is what I'm not sure of. Educating us about what? That half-inflated red rubber balls hurt when they hit you in the face? I knew that long before experiencing it. I may not be the world's deepest thinker, but even I have that much logic. What else does it teach? That all the varsity football players always seem to be on the same team in phys ed's touch football games? And they always forget to just touch you when you've got the ball? What it does teach us is that most of us are not going to win any gold medals at the Olympics. Unless they give one for playing dead during dodge ball. The competition for that gold medal would be unbelievable.

Phys ed often makes us feel clumsy, unathletic, and at times a little wimpy. But that's not the worst thing about phys ed class. Nope, compared to what's coming next, dodge ball seems downright enjoyable. The worst thing is something we all have to face—male and female, though not at the same time in the same place: the infamous phys ed shower.

"Hit me please, as hard as you can. Send me to the local emergency room if you have to. Just make sure I don't have to go to the SHOWERS."

A phys ed class without a shower is like *M* without *TV*. It just doesn't happen. It doesn't matter whether you played or sat in the bleachers, you're required to take a shower. I suppose that's so everyone will take at least one a week—the administration evidently fearing some of you are not smart enough to do it without any prompting from them. (Judging from the way the guy whose locker was next to mine in school smelled, that may be a realistic concern.)

The worst part about the shower is not the shower itself. It's not that difficult to stand under a nozzle and let water spray all over you. Most of you have been taking them for years. You just adjust the water, stand under it, soap up, rinse, get out, dry off, and get dressed. The last part of that last sentence gives a clue as to what makes phys ed showers so bad. Think about it. If, after a shower, you have to get dressed, it follows that while taking the shower you were not dressed. To put it more simply, you were naked. Nude. In the buff. Wearing nothing but your birthday suit. *That's* the worst part.

It's not that you've never been naked before. In fact, your parents probably have pictures of you running around as uncovered as a baby bird and not even seeming to mind it. They always get them out when you bring a new boyfriend or girl friend home for the first time. Of course you were only two or three at the time. And modesty was just a word to be learned in a far off future. But it's still embarrassing. It does prove that being naked is nothing new to you. You had no Calvin Kleins on in the delivery room. What's bothersome is that all those other people are naked at the same time you are. And they are all looking at you—because you are *naked.* At least that's how it seems. And being naked, with your body on display like a mannequin in a Sears window, everyone can see how you are—or aren't—built. And you can see how they are. And it seems that their parents did a better job of putting them together than yours did with you.

It's really mortifying.

We're all too aware of our bodily shortcomings, and here in the phys ed shower we have to parade them in front of everyone. We'll try anything to avoid it. We wear gym clothes into the shower saying they were dirty and needed cleaning too. Or we lather up all the "important parts" before reaching the shower. None of this works. Suddenly we're in the shower with Steve Stud or Suzy Sexy and we begin to feel less than inadequate. After all, everything around us, be it TV, magazines, movies, or whatever, shows us people with what the world considers perfect bodies. They are never too short or too tall, too thin or too fat, padded in all the wrong places, and all the other stuff we are. On a scale of one to ten they are all tens while we feel like minus-fives.

Being a teenager is hard enough without having to show off your bod to all the guys or girls in the freshman class. But there is good news. You need to remember that *everyone* is just as self-conscious as you. Even if they don't act like it. And if they're not, they probably should be. The perfect body doesn't exist. The guy or girl who seems to have one, probably has the IQ of a brick. Well, to be honest, they may be smarter than you are, too, but sometimes it's nice to think you've got them in one area. That's not the point. The point is that you are you and that's something to be proud of. Really it is.

We all have our problems. Even the tens get lonely, scared, flunk tests, and so on. You are special and unique. God made you special. The way you look has nothing to do with what you're worth. The way you are inside does. You can't easily control what you look like, but you can control what you are like.

So don't be discouraged as you trudge toward the phys ed shower and its ever-present towels sewn together from old sandpaper, and the scalding water and powdered soap. Everybody else is as nervous as you are. Look up and be confident. Be glad you are who you are. The outside, though we may wish it looked different, is only wrapping for the real person. The inside is what's important. It's what makes you you—someone special.

BIOLOGY

Biology emphasizes the nature of life, continuity of life, and the unique properties of living organisms that set every creature apart from the nonliving. The course involves the learner in the work of a scientist, developing skills and ideas in investigating biological phenomena. Emphasis will be placed on the observations and experiments that form the basis of our present understanding. Topics stressed include microbiology, botany, metabolism, genetics, and comparative anatomy.

• • • •

Mr. Burleson: Karleen, do you have your term paper on the belly of a frog?
Karleen: Well, no. I had some problems.
Mr. Burleson: Oh really? What?
Karleen: Well, first of all I had a hard time getting the frog in the typewriter . . .
Mr. Burleson and rest of class: Yecchhhh!!
Karleen: And then it croaked!

• • • •

There is nothing like the joy of scientific discovery. Now that you're a high schooler you are finally going to get to move into the realm of true science—the kind that brought forth space travel, atomic energy, and Cherry Coke. Grade school science was rather elementary stuff, looking at rocks and trees and telling which one was alive and which one wasn't. Sometimes you even got the answer right.

Whereas in the lower grades everything remotely scientific (like growing plants from a fourth of a potato stuck full of toothpicks and sitting in a mayonnaise jar) was lumped together in the science course, in high school you have choices of what to take. Now you can get barely passing grades in your choice of biology, physics, or chemistry. If you want to, you can sign up and almost fail them all.

Each course has unique characteristics that attract certain

43

students. If you take enough science, you eventually get to one you like. Putting together the stuff to make plastics explosives and blow up the school comes in chemistry. Contructing a working hang glider to catch an updraft and escape English will be taught in physical science. But first there's biology.

If you think the course description was interesting reading, then you'll love what the dictionary has to say about it.

bi-ol-o-gy: 1. the science that deals with the origin, history, physical characteristics, life processes, habits, etc. of plants and animals.

What that translates to in high-schoolese is that you're going to learn the difference between plants and animals— usually by cutting them open. That's not too bad with a plant. After all, when's the last time you heard a plant cry out in pain? ("Oh my gosh, Sean, did you hear that philodendron over there scream when Meagan cut into it?") With a fern you're relatively safe. Plus, they don't bleed much. Oh, maybe a little green ooze like something from "The Attack of the Man-Eating Cacti of Planet ZX" you saw on satellite TV from Japan at four o'clock one morning. But nothing major.

Then come the animals you have to dissect. That's biology talk for cut open and peer around inside of. You're safe with them too—at least that's what they tell you. They're all supposed to be dead, floating in jars of stuff called formaldehyde. They don't seem to be breathing. But still, they look just like the worms and frogs you used to carry home in your pants pockets.

Usually you start off with an earthworm. That's what the biology teacher tells you it is. You've never seen a fisherman put one of these on his hook. They are almost always the size of a small rattlesnake. With your luck you'll get a rattlesnake they put there by mistake.

The next thing they do is show you a chart of the internal organs of a worm, all color-coded for easier display. You memorize the chart (especially the colors) and then pick up your scalpel, put the worm in the tray with the wax bottom, and begin surgery. Or, rather, autopsy. That's when you get your first surprise. Nobody told the worm it was supposed to have all its major organs color coded. You think, *I must have gotten a bad one.* So you look around. If you got a defective dead worm, so did everybody else. None of the stuff that was supposed to be in color is. The science teachers and chart makers forgot to tell God to color those earthworm innards when He made them. So He didn't. Everything looks the same—a pinkish, brownish, reddish, grayish gooey mess. Like the lunches the kid next to you always seems to bring. The organs all look alike—real gross. But being the good scientist you are, you press on. Trying not to throw up.

After dismembering earthworms (which is fairly simple as they don't have arms, legs, or other appendages), you graduate to frogs. This is when the faint of heart fall out fast. Even the macho men, who like to make girls scream with their tales of terminating toads with the tires of their Toyotas, slither silently to the floor when the formaldehyde frog is fricasseed with their scalpel. Oh, there are those young Frankensteins who seem to love cutting things open. They're really scary, especially when you hear them suddenly begin a deep-throated, evil-sounding laugh that would make Stephen King cringe.

At last the class period is about to end. Time to put the dissecting tray and tools away. You close the door, go to the rest of your classes, then go home and dream about zillions of mutilated frogs slithering out of the school dumpster and heading for your bedroom—their ghostly "ribbits" resounding in your private nocturnal horror film. They are all coming to get you because of what you did to them.

Naturally, the school counselor, that dear saint who decides where you'll go when, has ensured that your biology class is right before lunch.

"Guess what we're having for supper tonight, Pamela, dear. Your favorite—frog legs and spaghetti!"

Yes, my friend, biology may look like fun, but sometimes you'll wonder why you're there at all. Well, watch out. You might learn something. Biology does tell us about God's creation, especially about the animate things (that's the living stuff like you, me, and the trees).

Biology can show us how fearfully and wonderfully we are made. It helps us realize just how complex we are. Did you ever try to help around the house and start to fix the TV set after little brother stuck the hamster in the back of it? Remember all the gadgets, doodads, and other weird wired stuff that lived in that genuine, simulated walnut-grained plastic cabinet? Well, we're even worse. We've got so much crammed into our flexible outer covering (also known as skin) that it's almost unbelievable. Believe it. Biology helps us.

Yes, biology class, in spite of all the nausea and gooey stuff, can tell us about the God who created all living things. It's pretty amazing how God thought it all up, put it all together, and made it work just right. From earthworms to frogs to you and me and the kid in the next seat with the funny-looking lunches. Biology makes you think about the One who put it all together in the first place. If you ask, then maybe the First Scientist will help you learn just what it is the biology teacher's after.

• LUNCH ••

MULLENVILLE
SCHOOL
LUNCH
MENUS

Mullenville—The Mullenville School Lunch
Menus for the week of May 19–23 are:

Monday—Hamburger Sandwich, Sliced
Pickles, Baked Beans, Banana, Peanut Butter
Cookie, Milk.

Tuesday—Chili Soup/Crackers, Peanut
Butter Sandwich, Tossed Salad, Blueberry
Cake, Milk.

Wednesday—Meat Loaf, Green Beans,
Celery Sticks with Peanut Butter, Sugar
Cookie, Milk.

Thursday—Sloppy Joe Sandwich, French
Fries, Corn, Peanut Butter Cake, Milk.

Friday—Pizza with Hamburger Topping,
Mashed Potatoes, Tossed Salad, Peanut
Butter Pie, Milk.

• • • •

Even if the first day of school is a little scary at least there is
one thing you can be sure of—lunch will be great. This is
something you can count on no matter what school you attend
or what part of the country you live in. School boards regularly
search the country for the world's finest chefs. Some even char-
ter flights to Paris and Rome's best schools of haute cuisine.
Only the finest cuts of beef, lamb, and pork are purchased.

Vegetables are trucked in daily. Fresh fruits are flown in from Florida and California. The waiters are well trained. The table service is finest silver, the china is imported, and the table-cloths are Ireland's best linen. Of course, the food is superb.

Actually it's not superb. It's pretty bad. There aren't any tablecloths, the table service is from U.S. Plastics Corporation, you are the waiter, and if there is a chef his name is Boy-ar-Dee. You never know what you're going to get. The school administration may print menus in the local paper and even post one on the cafeteria bulletin board, but none of that makes any difference. What we are talking about here is the difference between what the menu says and what it is you get. It may tell you what you are eating, and the cooks may even believe that what they are serving is what the menu says, but once you get your tray of food you won't really be sure what it is.

After all, how can you be? You can't ask anyone in authority. None of them are around. The teachers and administrators are all brown bagging it in the teachers' lounge—which ought to tell you something. And the way the cafeteria workers quickly stuff McDonald's and Wendy's sacks into the trash bins should be a clue, too. If none of these people eat the stuff they're fixing, why should you?

There are two ways you can have a school meal just like Mom would make. The first is to have Mom make it and send it with you in your Snoopy lunch box—which you've been carrying since second grade (and been trying to get rid of since third). You could even carry it in a brown paper bag, like the teachers do. (I know you think the teachers aren't too bright, but *you're* eating in the cafeteria and they're not. Think about it.) The second way is if your Mom is the school cook. If that's true you are either one of the thinnest people in your school or your taste buds died when you were an infant.

Actually school cooks are quite creative in the culinary arts. Many of them know at least 1,001 ways to ruin hamburger.

But back to the food. Have you ever wondered why the stuff tastes so bad? Of course you have. And after months of investigative reporting (during which I did not go so far as to actually *eat* in any school cafeterias, I mean, I did my time and got paroled, er, um, graduated), I can now report to you what actually goes into school food. Have lots of Pepto-Bismol ready before you read any further.

The first thing you need to know is that all of the ingredients are government surplus. That's right, stuff they couldn't give away. The armed forces couldn't use it, starving nations turned it down, and now they are making school meals out of it. Surplus peanut butter for example. I know you've tried to eat it. It's not like Jif or Peter Pan or even that oily, lumpy natural stuff that your mom buys at the local granola store. Surplus peanut butter has the consistency of six-day-old oatmeal and doesn't taste nearly as good. The school cooks use it for everything. Peanut butter sandwiches, peanut butter and jelly sandwiches, peanut butter and dill pickle sandwiches, peanut butter cookies, peanut butter ice cream, repairing broken steam pipes, and tuck-pointing broken bricks.

If the peanut butter isn't bad enough, there's the surplus white bread. Good old (emphasis on the *old*) white bread. The scary thing is that it's made out of the same ingredients you used to make paste out of in the first grade. White wheat flour and water. The stuff the kid next to you used to eat while pasting colored paper together. Then the teacher would yell at him, "Oh yucky! You ate that paste. Don't ever do that, it'll gum up your insides and you'll die." Now the teachers in the upper grades at school are telling you to eat it. What do they know that Mrs. Pamarr in grade school didn't?

There are a lot more things I could tell you about the secret ingredients of school lunches—like those 1,001 ways they use hamburger and what it's *really* made of. There may be some things you could tell me. I doubt that either of us wants to know. We would just as soon be grossed out on our own. Let lunch remain a surprise.

That's not all bad—surprises that is, not the food. Surprises can be fun. Like the fellow in John 5:1–9 who sat for thirty-eight years by a pool in Jerusalem waiting to be healed from a crippling disease. As the story went at that time, an angel used to come down and stir the water and the first one who made it in got healed. This fellow had been there all that time and never made it in at the right minute. If ever there was a person who knew what was going to happen it was this man. He'd been there for years. Nothing ever happened to him. Life held no surprises. Then along came Jesus. He healed the man. Talk about surprises.

Just like you have come to count on the cafeteria consumables being consistently crummy, this guy had come to count on being crippled. And until he met Jesus, who is full of surprises, he was. After that he was a new person. The story tells us he got up and walked away—never to be the same again.

So remember that man whenever the sameness of the cafeteria food is getting to you. He thought his life would never change. But it did. You never know. The cafeteria food could surprise you some day. It might actually be good. If it is, think about the One who surprised the crippled man by making him whole. If you let Him come by where you are He may just have some surprises in store for you. *Bon appetit.*

This course offers the college-bound student a broadened understanding of the major political forces in the world. Emphasis will be focused on the United States, the European powers and their Asian counterparts of the modern era, with time allotted for reference to Latin America, Africa, and the Middle East. This course should encourage understanding of world civilization and appreciation of the roots of American culture.

• • • •

Mr. Link: Now class, can anyone give me one year and tell the total tonnage of coal shipped from the United States in that year? Yes, Mike, what's your answer?
Mike: 1492—none.

• • • •

History class. Loved by few, hated by many. It appears to be full of facts and figures we can't comprehend. Names and dates come swirling at us from the mists of time gone by. Most of us cannot grasp the importance of the Battle of Agincourt, why it happened, where it happened, who it happened to, and what that has to do with us today. History is something that happened a long time ago to a bunch of people whose names we often can't pronounce and wouldn't want to in the first place. Some of them seem to have been pretty nasty characters. Certainly our folks wouldn't let us run around with someone named Attila, even if his mother did call him "Hon." Yet the teachers keep sending us things to memorize. Dates, places, names, causes. They want us to know what the U.S. in U.S. Grant's name stands for. The guys cruisin' McDonald's don't care. Teachers want us to understand why everyone got so upset that they started a war when Archduke Ferdinand and his wife got shot. That was *years* ago—before our parents even. The history that concerns us is who won the big game last Friday night and what it was that happened to make Julie and Dave stop talking to each other. *That's* history.

Yet from the time we were first graders, teachers have been trying to pound that stuff into heads that just don't care. We get world history, American history, state history, and city history. When we're little they put them all together. As we get older, the classes get more specialized: East African History, the History of Downtown Plainfield from 1941 to the Present, and so on. It is hard to imagine why anyone thinks all this old stuff is so important.

But it is. It's history, after all, that tells us how we, individually and as a nation and world, got to where we are. It tells us about the people of the past and shows us why they did the things they did. It shows us the mistakes people living before us made. Which may keep us from making them all over again. History also shows that though we should learn from it and keep from making those same mistakes again, we often don't.

History is more than dates and places from the past. It's about people. People like us. People who were young, who had dreams and aspirations. Like you, they were teenagers once. They fell in love. And out of love. Put them in a time machine, a pair of Levis, an Izod golf shirt, some Nikes, have their hair styled, and next thing you know they'd have a locker next to yours. People from the past are just that—people who happened to live in the past.

Someday you'll join them. In being history, that is. That's another important thing about history—you're making it now. How we live our lives today affects the lives of those in the future, just like the lives from the past affect us. The old line "Do that again and you're history" isn't an idle threat, you already are.

Lots of us avoid reading the Bible because we look at it as a history text. We've always thought of history books as boring. And while the Bible is about history, it's about an exciting kind. It's about how God interacts with His people. Us. Like regular history, it's about real people. Because it's from so long ago it's hard to imagine King David as a teenage music star or Mary as a young unwed mother-to-be, but they were. The people of the Bible were people just like us. They started out as babies, fell down a lot learning to walk, went to school, skipped school on spring days, fell in love, and on and on. Their history is special, because it's the history of God being involved with people.

That's what makes the Bible unique among books that have history in them. It's not a book about human exploits. It's about how God deals with us tiny humans. And when you stop to think about the mighty Creator of the universe wanting to be involved with us, it can be rather mind-boggling. The Bible, and its history, show us that God cares about us and our lives.

History may seem dull and uninspired. When it does, remember the Bible and its stories of God and humans. How God made us, loves us, and wants the best for our lives. It may be old news, but it's still the best news.

• EXPLORING ART ••

This is the introductory course for the entire art program and is required of all high school students before electing other courses. Emphasis is placed on drawing and painting, with some time also being given to ceramics, metalsmithing, silk-screening, and the like.

• • • •

Leon: Say, Mr. Guzzo, what do you think of this painting of my girl friend?

Mr. Guzzo: Well, it's not too bad. I mean, she's a cute girl and a good subject, but well, it just lacks something. Something's wrong with the smile. Where are her eyebrows? The lighting is kind of crazy, too. I know your mom thinks you paint really well, but to be honest, I think you ought to switch to Industrial Arts or something else. Your painting lacks finesse. Let's face it, Da Vinci, you'd probably be better off painting fences.

• • • •

Art class. Sounds like a good way to avoid sitting through another boring study hall, doesn't it? After all, you usually sit and draw on notebook paper to pass the time. Why not do it on art paper and get a good grade for the effort? Plus there are paints to play with, clay to kiln, and how hard can it be? I'll tell you. It's hard. Difficult. Really hard and difficult.

Artistic ability is like athletic ability: Either you've got it or you don't. If you don't, how are they supposed to teach it to you? Of course, you don't realize the disaster you've let yourself in for until it's too late. You remember art as that nice place in elementary school where you pasted colored paper and made uneven drinking cups from clay. Your mother and dad loved them. Your mom still has the clay cup sitting on the hutch at home.

"This is the little cup Bill made when he was in the third grade. Isn't it darling?"

You wish she'd throw it away. But she loves it and the teacher gave you an A. So you sign up for Exploring Art. After a couple of weeks with an art teacher who makes drill sergeants at boot camp seem downright lovable, you feel like you should have registered for Exploring Surgery—to find out where your brain was when you signed up for art.

You try to do a good job but realize your hands and mind don't seem to be on the same planet, let alone working together. And art teachers are quick. They can tell you're not doing well. They *know* what a bowl of flowers is supposed to look like. So you have a conference with the teacher. You know what a conference with a teacher is, don't you? That's when you meet with her and she tells you what you're not doing right. Finally you defend yourself. "I can't be an artist," you say. "I can't even draw a straight line." And the art teacher always says, "To be an artist you don't have to be able to draw a straight line. If you want to draw straight lines, get a ruler and go to drafting class. Art is being able to translate what the mind sees onto the medium." You feel better. It sounds good. Too bad it doesn't always work that way.

Let's be honest—face the problem head-on. We can't always make the paint, pen and ink, or clay do what we want it to. That's been true since we were little. When we started out all we had to try to do was stay inside the lines. At first we couldn't do that. Then slowly, by about the time we were in first or seventh grade, depending on our coordination, we could. But most of us can't make a face look like we all know faces should. The nose is always off-center or the head looks like it was hit with the flat side of a shovel. Still lifes are no better because the color of fruit in our rendition is further from real life than the artificial stuff at Grandma's house. And she's had it since 1935.

Then there are all the weird phrases about art. *Still life*, for one. What's it mean? Does it mean the fruit still has life? Or that the life is sitting still? And the tools they make you use. *Palette knives* for example. Did you ever try to cut open a palette with one of those? It just doesn't work. Don't ever get in a gang fight with one either. "Okay, Rocky, stand back or I'll work you over with my palette knife." Talk about fear and trembling. You'd better hope you can run fast. And *kilns.* Why don't they just call them what they are? Ovens. And *medium*—why doesn't the art teacher just call it paper, or paint, or clay, or whatever it is you're using? And if the jargon doesn't get you, the art teacher will, as shown earlier.

Art teachers have somehow come up with the idea that you will learn to paint like Picasso and everyone will find out that they taught you and you will get rich and make them famous. That's what they hope anyhow. And so whilst you are busy doodling and dreaming they will sneak up on you.

"What have you got there, Darren?"

"Well, uh. . . ."

"Why, that's a super start. I can see the beginning of buildings . . . their massive framing holding up an urban landscape filled with despair, overpopulation—seething with turmoil and hatred. It's amazing. It's powerful. Keep at it, Darren."

"Say, Darren, what was she rambling on about?"

"Hey, beats me. I was half-asleep and didn't see her coming."

But then you go on and finish the masterpiece based on your teacher's delusion of what you're doing and other art teachers around the city and state see your work and, being blessed with the same vision as your teacher, award your work first place in the state. Then you get caught up in the fervor, actually believing that Michelangelo is going to get a run for his reputation. Of course, you never do that well again and so go back to looking out windows and daydreaming.

Art class has its ups and downs. You do things you enjoy and things you hate. One time you're flinging clay with the best of them, the next you're cleaning brushes in turpentine and your boyfriend makes nasty remarks about your smelling like a paint store.

Art class can teach us an appreciation for the great Artist

who put this world together. As we look at the complexity of color, the subtlety of shading, and delicacy of lighting—none of which we can ever seem to duplicate in any of our assignments—we can come to appreciate God's artistic ability. Imagine the Soul who came up with the magnificent multitude of hues that color our lives. We realize that God must like beauty too, since He made so much of it.

So if you're frustrated at getting too much fresco in your messco, stop. Take a look around. And thank God that it was He—not you—who put it all together. You might even want to let Him know you think He deserves an A for the finished product. Even if you aren't an art teacher.

Mr. Morgan: Excuse me, Tim, but what are you doing crawling up and down the corridor and looking at it so closely?
Tim: Well, I looked at my schedule to see what I was supposed to do this period and it said "study hall."

• • • •

Study hall. An example of false advertising (see Consumer Economics) if there ever was one. It's forty-five minutes or so when you don't study and it's held in a room, not a hall. Let's look at the hall part first.

When you first hear that you've got a study hall, you get a little worried. And you should be. Years of educational conditioning have taught you that if you do anything bad they'll send you out in the hall.

"Michelle, if you don't stop passing those notes, you're going out in the hall."

"John, if you're going to insist on talking to Willy, it's out in the hall with you."

So you wonder what it is you've done, before the first day of class even, that has caused them to send you out in the hall to study. Then you find out—you're not out in the hall, you're in the auditorium or some other huge room. Talk about a relief. You grab your books, notebooks, pencils, three-ring binders, and anything else you can carry and trudge off to study hall. When you get there it looks as if every other freshman is in there at the same time. In order to keep order they space you out. No, I don't mean with drugs or anything, I mean seating arrangements. There are five seats and three rows between you and the next person. This is so you will study and not sit around whispering. So you don't. Either. You don't study and you don't whisper. You *yell.* Whispering won't do any good

62

over these kind of distances. Besides, how do they expect you to study when they've got guards watching every move you make? I know they call them teachers, but the only other place you'll see people built like them is on "Big Time Wrestling." If they teach anything it's big time wrestling and study hall. Just having them walking around the room, constantly clearing their throats, sounding like trucks backfiring, and glaring at you like you're an ax murderer is enough to keep you from studying. No wonder you talk to your distant neighbor. You may want to plan an escape from the place before the end of the period.

"Yes, Governor Wilson, we've got a prisoner, I mean student, riot in Study Hall A—I think we should call in the National Guard."

Have you ever tried to figure out why study hall was invented? The official reason is that kids need a place to get a head start on their homework assignments. In reality it's a place developed by a top secret government project dealing with all the things adults can't figure out. Things like new model paper airplane designs, how far a penny will roll before being stepped on by a study hall monitor, and how many pages of *Mad* magazine can be read before a teenager is caught. Everyone knows that very few books are opened—and then, only if there's something hidden inside them, like a sandwich or *Sports Illustrated.*

The *hall* part is not the only misleading misnomer. How about *study?* You can't do it there. The atmosphere is all wrong. How can they seriously expect anybody to study in such a sterile setting? How are you supposed to get your algebra done without Pat Benatar's help? Get real. Or study history without "Leave It to Beaver"? It's hopeless. There are too few distractions to be able to get any work done. If they want you to study they ought to a least turn on some big screen TVs or play "Q-97—The Rock of Richmond" or something.

Real studying can only be done amongst clutter and chaos.

The preferable setting is at the kitchen table at about 5:30 P.M. Mom is trying to get supper on, little brothers and sisters are playing hide-and-seek in the kitchen cabinets, Dad is changing light bulbs in the ceiling fixture, the TV is tuned to "Voltron," and you're listening to Quiet Riot on your Walkman. Your assignment is to come up with something easy like how much the earth should weigh at midnight next Tuesday, taking into consideration changes in the population, the way the sun's rays will strike downtown Sydney, Australia, and stuff like that. Now that's an optimal educational atmosphere. If schools could find a way to duplicate that kind of ambience, then study halls would succeed.

Alas, if just can't be done. Oh, your fellow students try to help out by raising the occasional ruckus. All they get for their pains is some more pain, usually administered by the assistant principal. But maybe, though we doubt it, study halls, with their quietness, can be beneficial.

Quietness makes us focus in on what we are doing. After all, there's nothing else to focus on. When we give our full attention to something we tend to learn more about it than we do when we've got one eye on the TV, one on the book, one ear to the stereo, and the other on the phone. If graduation is one of your goals, and I'm sure it is, then focusing on schoolwork is not all bad.

Quietness is something we need in our spiritual life, too. We need time to get alone, away from the hustle, bustle, and busyness. Jesus did that a lot. Like the time we read about in Matthew 14:23. Jesus had just fed over five thousand folks— and done that after preaching to them all day. He sent the disciples on ahead and He "went up the hillside quite alone" (PHILLIPS). That's just one of many times. The Bible tells us of a lot more. If Jesus, with all His power, thought getting away alone with God was important, maybe we should too.

When we're alone with God, sitting quietly, we may be able to hear Him talk to us. Often we're so busy that even our prayers are a bit noisy. We tell God what we want and then don't hang around to hear the reply.

If we want God's help in living our lives, we have to get quiet long enough to hear Him talking to us. After all, Christians are in a relationship with God. And just as our earthly relationships need two-way communication to stay healthy, so does our heavenly one.

The next time you're in study hall and the quiet is getting to you, let it. Use the time to really be quiet. Listen to God. You might learn something in study hall.

(f-150)

This is a course in developing skills and forming good habits in speaking. The major part of the time is spent in developing listening and speaking habits, with reading and writing of lesser importance. Spanish is used in the classroom except when lengthy explanations need to be given.

• • • •

La Profesora: Buenos días, classe.
Los Estudiantes: Buenos días, profesora.
La Profesora: ¿Dónde está sus lecciones?
Juan: Está en me casa.
La Profesora: ¿Por qué?
Juan: ¿Escusa me?
La Profesora: ¿Por qué?!
Juan: ¿Escusa me?
La Profesora: ¿Por qué?!
Juan: Butter.
La Profesora: Okay, young man, now you can butter yourself down to the principal's office and see how funny *he* thinks you are.
Juan: ¿Por qué?

• • • •

Ah, the joys of learning a foreign tongue. If you're like most people there will be times you will wish you had a foreign tongue because your English one just won't make the sounds your Spanish, French, German, or whatever teacher wants it to make. "Trill your Rs," she'll say, and the only way you can do it is by making your tongue do things your mother told you she'd smack you for if you ever did them again. So you haven't for years. Now some adult is upset with you because you won't go against all those years of Mom's threats.

In addition to doing things with your mouth that would

cause you grievous bodily harm if you did them at home, there are some things you would get in trouble for if you did them in other classes at school. In Spanish you are told to pronounce your *E*s like long *A*s and your *I*s like long *E*s. If you did that in English class, the teacher would throw you out.

Mrs. Gosney: Laura, would you please recite the assigned poem for us at this time?

Laura: E theenk that E shall navar say,
    A poam lovaly as a tray.

Mrs. Gosney: That's quite enough, young lady!
Where did you learn such awful pronunciation?

Laura: Why, from Mrs. Hernandez in Spanish class.

When you first think about it, learning a foreign language should be a ball. You'll be able to amaze your parents and grandparents with your newfound ability to mumble not just in English but also in a language they can't understand.

Papa: What's that you say, Eric? I don't seem to understand a word you're saying.
Eric: Excuse me, *Papa,* I was merely conversing with myself in *français*—I mean, French.
Papa· Oh, I'm sorry, I thought you were mumbling again.
Eric: *Au contraire, Papa,* just doing my homework.
Papa: That's a good fella. Say, Barbara, how about that son of ours? Some linguist, right?!

Of course, you know you were only mumbling stuff that wouldn't get you an *A* in class, but it fooled the folks.

If you get really good there may even be a career in foreign service where you'll meet all kinds of exotic people, live in weird-sounding places, and eat things that you're not sure you want to know what they are.

But enough of the glamour. You know you're in trouble when classes begin. The old alphabet and punctuation marks were hard enough and now these foreign languages want you to add some new signs. Things like "~" or "^" or upside-down exclamation points and question marks. If you've decided to get really exotic and study Russian or Chinese or some such thing, you don't have to worry about the ~s and ^s. No, there you get to learn a whole new alphabet. One that looks like something off of a planet from *Star Trek XXIII—The Search for the Searchers of Spock*. And you thought English was tough.

That's only the beginning. Then come all those weird tenses—past plu-imperfect present third-person multiple or whatever. You can't even remember the English ones well enough to talk to your elderly aunt who keeps reminding you to speak precisely and "E-nun-ci-ate!" And the teacher wants you to keep in mind regional dialects and tenses so you can negotiate world peace with a Tibetan nomad?

And what are you supposed to do when you don't understand something? In any other class you would ask a question. Don't try it here, it won't work. Why? Because the teacher won't speak to you in anything but the foreign language. If you knew the language well enough to ask a question in it, you probably wouldn't have to even ask it anyhow, now would you? What's a kid to do?

At least language lab looks like fun. You get to put on the headphones and listen to tapes. Too bad they're not John Cougar Mellencamp or Aretha Franklin. The tapes just go on saying the same things over and over and over and over and over and over. "¿Donde está la cafeteriá? . . . ¿Donde está la cafeteriá? . . . ¿Donde está la cafeteriá? . . ." This goes on for hours. At least it seems like hours when your rear end is starting to go to sleep from those molded plastic chairs they make you sit on. For a while you repeat along with the tape. But after two thousand "¿Donde está la cafeteriá?"s you begin pretending you're Luke Skywalker with Han Solo giving you target coordinates so you can atomize Darth Vader's Ti-fighter or a big-time radio deejay programming the most popular Top 40 show in town.

"Hey, dudes and chicas, this is Benny the
Blaster comin' at you with nonstop,
uninterrupted, commercial-free totally
terrific Top 10 tracks for the next
twenty-five days straight!!"

Then comes test time. You realize instead of playing *Star Wars* you should have stuck to *Language Wars* because you just got a *D−*.

Foreign language is a challenge. That's why they call it foreign. If it came easily it wouldn't be so foreign to your learning processes. But, as hard to believe as it may be, after a while you'll begin to understand some of it. Then a little more of it. Then a lot. Soon you and your friends will be making jokes in Upper Voltian and only the other Upper Voltian students will get them. And laugh. The rest of the folks will just think you're weird. But you know better. They are jealous because you just told the funniest joke in the world and none of them got it. Or even could get it. Slowly your grades will start to improve. That may not be as neat to you as being able to tell great jokes, but your parents will love it. And anything you do that your parents love will help you greatly when you want to borrow the car come Friday night.

Most amazing of all, years later, when your plane touches down in Upper Volta, words and phrases you hadn't thought of for years will begin to come back to you as soon as you hear the natives speaking them. If you've been speaking it all along it will be like second nature to you and you will finally be able to communicate well enough to find out why your luggage went to Lower Volta.

Praying is like learning a foreign language. At first it seems hard. For some of us, it doesn't just seem hard, it *is* hard. You sit in church, listening to someone else praying and the words come so easily and beautifully. Then *you* try it. Your words are hardly out of your mouth and they fall to the ground like a cement block. How will you ever be able to do what Paul tells you to do—pray without ceasing? You'd rather cease without praying.

With prayer as with foreign language, practice and patience work wonders. Stick to it. Try to pray the way you feel most comfortable. Remember, no one is grading you. You're talking to God, and He's so glad for the chance to chat with you He's not even watching for perfect grammar. It's a conversation with Someone who really does want to spend time with you. Pretty soon it will begin to come naturally. After all, prayer is just a talk between humans and God. It's something we need to learn to do if we ever want it to be natural. We're the ones who make it foreign. Like any language we have to keep using it to be able to use it well.

When you're sitting in language lab, listening to the tape, about to give it all up, give up a prayer instead. Your foreign language grade probably needs the prayer—and you need the practice.

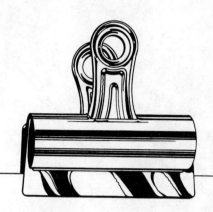

MULLENVILLE SCHOOL DISTRICT
Official Class Schedule

Thomas	John	Alan	10	326
(last)	(first)	(middle)	(grade)	(homeroom)
123 Pleasant Valley Lane		Mullenville	555-5555	1125
(street)		(city)	(phone)	(locker)

Class	Code	Room	Mon.	Tues.	Wed.	Thurs.	Fri.
Geometry	m–340	114	X	X	X	X	X
Phys Science	s–425	326	X	X	X	X	X
English 10	e–040	212	X	X	X	X	X
Lunch		caf					
Exp Shop	i–627	101	a–111	X	a–111	X	a–111
Consumer Econ	ec–273	322	X	X	X	X	X
Journalism	e–140	218	X	X	X	X	X
Study Hall			main auditorium				
Health	p–896	118	X	s–41	X	s–41	s–41

Note: Numbers appearing in weekly schedule indicate study hall seat assignments.

• GEOMETRY ••

This course is for the college-bound student. Logical reasoning is slowly but steadily developed from geometric proofs until the student gains an appreciation of the value of the methods of inductive and deductive reasoning. Because of the broad view, this course will be of value to many students not only for training in reasoning habits, but also for the general knowledge of material covered which is useful in everyday life.

• • • •

Mr. Durham: Will someone please explain the beginning steps in measuring a plane?
Chad: First you catch a cab to the airport, then . . .

• • • •

Reread the course description. Now repeat after me—"Huh?!" This course description seems even more goofy and unintelligible than the ones from the English department. Perhaps it's because math teachers are goofier than English teachers. But that's pretty hard to believe. I do think they speak a different language than the rest of us humans though. Maybe if we look at it line by line we can make some sense of it. Let's try.

"College-bound student." What exactly is a *college-bound student?* That's sort of scary. *College-bound* sounds like a bunch of Yale admissions counselors dressed like Indians have swooped down on some sad sophomore who really wants to go to Harvard and tied him to an anthill until he changes his mind. Not a pretty picture, you must admit.

I think what they mean, though, is someone who is planning on going to college. They are *bound for college.* What a relief.

Then there's "logical reasoning." They've got to be kidding. What's the fun of that? That's the stuff your parents are always using on you.

"Use your head, for heaven's sake! [Author's note: I've always wondered how anything I did as a teenager made much difference in heaven's behalf.] Even your two-year-old sister can logically see that what you want to do is the dumbest thing a human has ever come up with."

Well, any other idiot may have been able to, but I never could. Aren't you glad the sentence also says "slowly but steadily"? In many of our cases, the emphasis better be on the "slowly" because we're not anywhere close to being sure what they mean by the phrase "methods of inductive and deductive reasoning."

"Wait! I've got it, Holmes. Reasoning is how you solve your cases, correct?"
"Brilliant deduction, Dr. Watson."

Good! Geometry is going to help us become private detectives. And you thought we might have to sign up for one of those correspondence courses in the back of *Unpopular Mechanics.*

Besides the final sentence sounding a lot like the run-on sentences they warned us about in English 9, I'm not too sure how much of this stuff is going to be "useful in everyday life." If they want to talk about spelling and English, okay. I believe that. People in our office use the dictionary every day, trying to figure out the spelling of some word they were supposed to have learned in the tenth grade. I've got one open right now while I'm writing this. I forgot how to spell *dictionary.*

But I can't tell you the last time someone said, "Quick, I need to find the altitude of an equilateral triangle whose side is twenty. Hand me *Geometry for Home and Office.*" Well, actually I can tell you—never. We don't even have a geometry book around. I had to go to the library and check one out just to come up with a problem for the sentence above.

Yet, logical reasoning can help us. God did give all of us a brain. Even if we do wonder about some people. It's a water-cooled, dual component, biological, analog computer. We're expected to use it. Logically. If we learn how to reason logically we can save ourselves a lot of trouble. We'll be able to look at the pros and cons of an action or situation. We can see the consequences. Or benefits. Logic can keep us from making horrible mistakes.

We all know people who are just like us but who have made real messes of some part of their lives. We may have even been able to see it coming. We said, "If they'd just open their eyes and see what's happening, they'd do something about it. Why don't they just *think* about what they're doing?" Maybe they didn't know how.

Therefore, when Mr. Biddle is standing at the blackboard, geometrising away, and you're tiring of Euclid (which you had always thought was just a suburb of Cleveland), logic, deduction, and induction, you might want to pay attention. Learning logical thinking might just help keep you from skinning your emotional knees. And you know how much skinned knees hurt.

Physical Science is designed to give a rigorous study of the physical principles and concepts of fundamental areas. Topics covered include the metric system, nuclear structure of the atom, nuclear energy, radioactivity, Newton's laws of forces as they relate to gravity, airplane flight, potential and kinetic energy, heat energy, electrical energy, and simple machines. Laboratory experiments are incorporated into this course.

• • • •

Mr. Kirk: Okay now, Jim, just what is it you are trying to do with that flashlight and telescope pointing in Jonathan's ear?
Jim: I'm trying to see if there's anything in there.
Mr. Kirk: Of course there's something in there. Why wouldn't there be?
Jim: Well, all I know is that yesterday you told us life couldn't exist in a *vacuum*.

• • • •

The dictionary says that physics is "the science dealing with the properties, changes, interactions, etc. of matter, and energy in which energy is considered to be continuous, including electricity, heat, optics, mechanics, etc."

That's almost as confusing as the course description's explanation of it. What all that scientific mumbo jumbo means is that physics deals with stuff that is not now and has never been alive. In other words, you are not going to be cutting up earthworms and frogs in this class. That might make some of you feel easier about taking it.

Instead you do lots of experiments in an attempt to come to an understanding of the laws of physics. One thing you do is put your hands on a Van de Graaff generator. That doesn't sound too bad. Until you see what it does to your classmates' hair. R. J. Van de Graaff was an American physicist (not to be confused with J. D. van der Waals, the Dutch physicist—and your parents were worried you wouldn't learn anything from this book) who invented an electrostatic generator that used a movable insulating belt in order to produce potentials of millions of volts. What that means is the potential to light you up so your descendants could stand you in a corner and read by you for the next two or three trillion years. Still think it doesn't sound too bad?

In physics class the teacher, with a gleam in her eye, asks for volunteers to come up and put their fingers on the machine. You're not to be alarmed that it looks like something from an old Frankenstein movie. Then, not waiting for anyone to volunteer, because she knows she would be there all period, she calls on you. Being the good kid you are, you go—all the while asking yourself quietly, *Don't condemned people normally get a last meal?* Finally, there you are, hands on top of the cold steel dome that sits on the generator. The switch is thrown. It begins to hum. Suddenly every hair on your body is standing straight out. She's created a monster! Then it is shut off. Your hair, at least most of it, goes back to where it's supposed to be. You've lived to tell about it.

What is the point of this experiment, you ask? Why, it's to prove the law of physics that if you put your hands on a Van de Graaf generator all of your hair will stand up. Any more silly questions?

Oh, you also learn things about static and kinetic energy. They teach you the difference between them by having you sit in a chair not doing anything. This shows you a body (yours), mass, or force at rest. That's *static*. Then the teacher asks for volunteers to come spin you around and around and around in the chair. This time everyone volunteers. They spin you around and around and around. Then you throw up. That's the energy of a body which results from its motion. Also known as *kinetic*. Aren't you glad you learned the difference?

Physics is a delightful, fun subject—especially if you are really into bodily injury. It's sort of like a demolition derby, with you as the car. Many life, health, and accident insurance policies are not in force while the insured (that's you again) is in physics class.

If you survive it—and many of you will—physics can show you the wonder of God's universe. An invisible thing like white light, or sunlight, is revealed to contain whole rainbows when seen through a prism. Electricity, something else we can't see, is shown to have almost magical force. We use physics every day to help us enjoy the life God gave us.

Physics does teach us that there are lots of laws governing our existence on this earth. Like the law of gravity. If it were ever revoked, we'd go zooming off into space like fireworks on the Fourth of July instead of plodding steadily along with both feet on the ground. Or the laws of aerodynamics—which allow aeronautical engineers to design planes that fly instead of fall. Or thermodynamics—the transformation of heat into other forms of energy. When the temperature hits minus five, we're glad someone came up with thermodynamics.

The nice thing about these laws is that they are constant. The law of gravity is not in effect one day and out the next. You can be sure when you get out of bed and put your feet on the floor you won't go flying out the window. (Although it would be nice if the law of gravity could be suspended for about five minutes the day you have to rake that backyard that suddenly grew into fifty acres. Just think of the possibilities. All the leaves go shooting up into the sky toward the sun. A kind of interstellar incinerator.) When you're flying in a plane, you can put your seat back back, put on the headphones, and be assured that the laws of lift won't be cancelled, with the result of you plummeting from thirty thousand feet above to about six feet below in the next few minutes. Those laws are good to know and have operating. You don't have to get up in the morning and call the Bureau of Physical Laws' 800-number to find out which ones are in and which ones are out that day.

Physical Science class and its constant laws also remind us of something else that is constant. God's love. In Romans 8 we're told that nothing can separate us from this love. It's always there. God is unchanging. We can depend on that. In a world where so much seems undependable, it's a good feeling to know there is something you can count on. The One who made these constant physical laws is constantly there for us. God loves you. Always has. Always will.

English 10 includes a study of the literature of America, selected fiction (short story and novel), drama, and poetry. Students will become acquainted with the works of Hawthorne, Whitman, Twain, and others. Another segment of the class covers basic composition skills including a review of grammar and the study of the development of good paragraphs. There will also be emphasis on expository writing. The purpose of this writing style is to inform and enlighten.

• • • •

Mr. Harding: Is there someone here who can use the word *fiction* in a sentence?
Ralph: I can. When my dad's tractor broke down, he spent the whole day *fic-shun* it.

• • • •

Once you've made it past ninth grade English, and understand the basics, they let you read things by real writers, not your classmates. You're moving from the minors to the majors. Big league wordsters are lining up at the plate for the chance to knock you out of the park of adolescent illiteracy into the adult world of *real* literature. No more Hardy Boys or Nancy Drew for you anymore. You'll now be playing shortstop of the short story. You've got to be quick—plots, subplots, characters, and motivations will be coming at you with the speed of a ball off Gary Carter's bat. You have now moved into the arena of fiction. You're ready, aren't you? You do know what fiction, is, don't you?

Okay, back to the dugout for a friendly manager-to-rookie talk from Coach Bill. It's simple. Fiction is stuff that's not true. Nonfiction is stuff that is true. Understand? I'm glad *you* do. It's always seemed backwards to me. To me, *non* was a clue that the stuff couldn't be trusted. *Non*dairy creamer means the liquid in that little container has never even been near a cow.

And it tastes like it. *Non*skid mat means you can now step into the shower without fear of hitting a slick spot and sliding out the window with nothing but some soap bubbles covering you. Now comes *non*fiction. I know it means "not fiction," but it sounds more like it shouldn't be true. But nonfiction is how it really is, while fiction is how it really ain't. It's my opinion that *fiction* and *nonfiction* ought to be dropped. Just call them stories or *non*-stories. Everyone knows what stories are. They are fun to read. Likewise, everyone knows what *non*-stories are—not fun to read. *Texas* by James Michener is story, or fiction. It's fun. *Geometry* by anybody is *non*-story, or nonfiction. It is also *non*-fun.

One of the things you were supposed to have learned in ninth grade was that if you aren't really sure of the definition of a word, you look it up in the dictionary. Although I'm partial to the above definitions of *fiction* and *nonfiction*, I've got a sneaking suspicion that not very many English teacher types would allow you to use them in a class discussion. So, to keep them happy and you in good grades (and show that I learned *my* language and library skills when I was in the ninth grade), let's see what the dictionary says about *fiction* and *nonfiction*.

Fiction/fik'-shən *n* [ME *ficcioun* < OFr. *fiction* < L. *fictio*, a making, counterfeiting < pp. of *fingere*, to form, mold] any literary work portraying imaginary characters and events, as a novel, story, or play.
Non-/non/ [L *non*, not < OL *noenum* < *ne-*, negative participle + *oinom*, one] a prefix meaning not: used to give a negative force, esp. to nouns, adjectives, and adverbs.

See, what did I tell you? Stories and non-stories. Made-up stuff and truth. My definitions may not have as much class as Mr. Webster's in the dictionary, but they are right.

We all like stories. At least we do until we take English 10. Our teachers' ideas of stories and ours then seem to run at cross angles—and rarely, if ever, intersect. We want to read *I*

Was a Teenage Rutabaga and they want us to read *Narrative of the Life of Frederick Douglass*. We rebel. After all, many of these stories are old. I mean *old*. Older than our parents. Older than our grandparents, even. Some of them are even older than our grandparents' parents. And yet, we begin to read. We read because we know we should. We read because it is going to stretch our minds. We read because we'll get an *F* if we don't.

It's painful at first. Not at all easy. The language, along with time and people, has changed. People in the stories don't say things like, "That's totally rad," or, "Gross me out the back door." Their phrases seem a bit stilted. But as we get into them, they start to come alive. We find ourselves slipping along the sea-washed deck, part of the crew sailing on the *Pequod* in search of the white whale named *Moby Dick*. We learn to sing songs of ourselves with Walt Whitman. We are ready to charge the front and display our *Red Badge of Courage*.

The stories come alive because, though we talk and dress differently, we feel the same things people felt long ago. Stories speak to us because they speak of human emotions. Just as we love and laugh and live, so did they. Story people share a commonality with us—even though we are real and they are imaginary.

At times, people in the Bible stories we've grown up with seem like that—imaginary. They're not. They are real. The tales of their lives make up some of the best literature of all time—fiction or non. Why? For the same reasons we can identify with people in stories. They're just like us. They succeed and they fail. They do what God wants one time and blow it the next. They walk and talk and feel the same ways we do. We've just come along a few thousand years later. Their stories remain, so that we might see ourselves in them and them in us. By so doing, we can see that the same ways God worked in their lives, He can work in ours. In that sense, the Bible stories are much more real than the stories we read in English 10. They are truth.

When you're wearily reading *Outcasts of Poker Flats* because you have to, remember that it's a story about people like you. And remember another Book that is full of stories about people like you. Maybe then, the Good Book will become a good book for you.

This course will instruct the student in uses of machinery, safety, and basic industrial arts skills. Students will complete a number of projects in drafting, woodworking, and metal shop. Finish work and quality of detail will be stressed.

• • • •

Mr. Carter: Today we are going to cut down those four oak trees out back, turn them into two-by-fours and two-by-sixes and siding, frame in the new addition to the school shop, side it, insulate and roof it, finish trim it, and paint it. Are there any questions? Yes, Amos, what is it?
Amos: Mr. Carter, sir, this is a one-hour class.
Mr. Carter: I know that, Amos, but don't worry, I'll find something for you boys to do for the other forty-five minutes.

• • • •

Shop class. Something every red-blooded American male has to live through at least once. Some red-blooded females, too. The first day of shop class is one of the best first days of a class you'll ever attend. At least mine was. About thirty-five girls were there. They had all shown up by mistake. They thought we were going to learn how to shop. One of them kept asking if they were going to take us out to the mall in a school bus or would we just shop by catalog. Their motto was the same as my friend Nancy's is: "When the going gets tough, the tough go shopping." By the time the year was over, I was wishing I had been one of the "tough." They (and the rest of us) soon found out that the only thing shop class had in common with the local mall was that our tools came from Sears.

Shop class, which is also called Industrial Arts (just why is undetermined, as it has hardly anything to do with industry and very few of the projects turn out artfully), is an adventure in learning. At least, that's what they tell you. That's teacher talk for "Boy, are you in over your head." You don't believe them. After all, you've been using, abusing, and losing your father's tools for years now. You've built tree houses, forts, go-karts, and all kinds of other useful gadgets. You know you are ready for the big time.

Shop is usually a combination of drafting, wood shop, and metal shop. This teaches you how to take the raw materials of wood, metal, and paper and turn them into completely worthless objects. Well, not completely worthless. Chances are your grandmother will love whatever it is you make and give her for Christmas.

The sequence of shop is important. The most common sequence is to take drafting first, then wood, and finally metal. That way you take one project from the design stage (drafting) to the throwaway stage (metal), utilizing the different aspects of each subject. My first year we ruined a planter.

The first day of shop our teacher showed us a beautiful rectangular planter that would be our project for the year. It was really pretty. He explained that we would first draw our own scale plans of it in drafting. Then we would go to wood shop and construct the walnut exterior. The last stop would be metal shop, where we would make the galvanized steel liner. Seeing such a fine piece of workmanship before us, and sure we could do as well, we set forth. We should have just set still.

Drafting class should have been easy. We struggled in art but here, finally, was a place where we could use pencils and rulers and T-squares and other objects to make straight lines. We still couldn't. We saw the shop instructor's work and couldn't come close. Our drawings were filled with graphite smudges and eraser marks. We stopped and drew it again. And again. And again. Until we—and the teacher—gave up, and we moved on to woodshop.

There he gave us bunches of odd-sized pieces of wood and showed us how to use the various tools around the shop. First there was the band saw. My first thought was, *What kind of band does it saw?* After I heard our school band, I knew the answer. Even if it was the wrong one. Then he showed us the electric plane. Now I'd heard of jet planes and propellor planes, but couldn't see how they'd make an electric plane.

Think of the extension cord you'd need. Then I found out it was used to plane off the wood you didn't want. Next we were shown the brace and bit. I'd always called it a drill. Then there was adhesive. That's shop talk for glue.

Finally, I'd band-sawed, planed, braced and bitted (or should that be just *bit* or *bited*? Maybe I should go back to English 9), and adhesived. By the end of the semester I had, though competition was tough, the ugliest walnut planter ever made at West High School. And there was still the liner waiting for me in metal shop. I was hoping that the school bus might explode on the way to school so I wouldn't have to finish.

Metal shop was not as bad as I feared. I learned a lot there. For instance, tin-snips not only cut galvanized steel, they also do nice work on copper pennies. And a forge is a good place to throw cut-up copper pennies when the shop teacher starts looking at you funny. Also it's sometimes easier to make a mistake with metal than with wood. At least, you don't have to wait for another tree to grow. I also learned that I was as bad a metalsmith as a woodworker.

When the year ended I had to take my planter home. I didn't really want to, but I did. I gave it to my mom. She oohed and aahed and thanked me. She didn't really want to, but she did.

As bad as I was at shop, there are those who are good. Some really excel. While some of us take a year to make a deformed planter, others turn out beautiful things. Lumps of metal and hunks of wood become desks and chairs or lamps and hutches. It's amazing what some people can do with the same materials I destroyed. It's fun to watch someone who has the ability to be a craftsman work with wood or metal. They can take something raw and make it refined.

It makes you think about the One who created the raw material. Consider for a minute the Craftsman who then took it and made it into something beautiful: the world and everything that's beautiful around us.

When you are about to take board in hand, to try to square

it for the twenty-fifth time (even though it's now too short to be usable) think about the One who made it all—without the help of drafting class, woodshop, or metal shop. From scratch. And who deserves an $A+$ for the finished product.

• CONSUMER ECONOMICS ••

(ec-273)

Consumer Economics assists students in examining and clarifying their values, interpreting and understanding data, and making informed choices concerning their life-styles, both in the near and distant future. This course provides opportunities for learning how to make informed decisions in the economy by introducing topics that match student interest by using local laws and tax issues, newspaper and magazine articles, television specials, and advertising as catalysts to provide learning opportunities. Students learn about the American economic system, how technology and resources on the local, state, national, and international levels affect them, and how changing events alter patterns of employment, levels of earning, and standard of living.

• • • •

Mr. Peacock: Now that our semester is about over, who can give me a one-sentence summary of what you've learned in Consumer Economics?
Kathleen: To buy or not to buy,
        That is the question.

• • • •

Consumer Economics is a course that teaches you how to buy things. What could be better? A class on spending money. Sounds like fun, doesn't it? After all, we all like to buy things. Some of us are born buyers. As my friend Nancy says, "I never met a dollar I couldn't spend." Now there's a course on it at school, and it actually counts toward graduation.

As you get into the class you find it's not all that simple. For one thing, they don't give you a thousand dollars or anything like that to spend any way you want at the Glendale Mall. Consumer Ec is more about *how* to do it than doing it.

Consumer Economics teaches you lots of things about consuming, though. You don't get to start with buying—even

95

pretend buying—you have to work up to that. Consumer Economic's premise is that you need to know what goes into the making and marketing of the consumer goods you want to consume before you consume them. Still consumed by the idea of this class? I thought not, but it's not as bad as it sounds.

You start out learning about manufacturing and marketing. You learn about truth in advertising. You find out that truth in advertising is about as common as lizard livers on the menu at McDonald's. You can have truth or you can have advertising, but rarely can you have both at the same time. I'm not convinced we consumers would really like it if we could. Think how boring the commercials, often some of the best programming on TV, would be.

> "Our new Toysanda is pretty good. It's radio is fair, the seats are nice, but it only comes in red or blue. It's better than some cars, but not as good as others. You really should look around before spending $12,000."

Not very exciting, huh? Not nearly as good as

> "Toysanda—the car that blows the doors off the competition!!! Drive one today and experience lightspeed! It's got an eighty-seven-speaker sound system that rivals Carnegie Hall. The seats were designed by surgeons and would be right at home in your living room. This special edition is made just for you in your choice of Firemist Red or Midnight Blue. Nowhere in the galaxy will you get more car for your money. Order yours today!!!!!"

That's a lot better. It may not be true—after all, you've seen Toysandas go down the road before, and they're all going fifty-five the same as you, and you haven't noticed any cars with their doors blown off sitting by the side of the road. But it *sounds* so much better. Consumer Economics tries to help you get beyond the hype of advertising. That way you know what you're getting.

Another way it does this is by showing you how products are made. To do this, you usually are told to do "market/product research" on a product. You are assigned something like hair dryers and then have to research how they are made, who makes them, what brand names are available, and how to decide whether you're buying a good one. I remember my "market/product research" project. It was on hot dogs. Doesn't sound very exciting, does it? Well, it turned out more exciting than I wanted it to be.

Like most teenagers, I lived on hamburgers, hot dogs, chips, and cola. That's probably why I was so healthy as a kid—all that junk food that my parents kept telling me was so bad for me was also bad for all the germs I encountered and killed them too. Then the Consumer Economics teacher tells me I have to do a report on how hot dogs are made. That was easy. I ate them all the time. I finished up the report before class was even over.

Making a Hot Dog
(A Report by Brent Bill
for Mrs. Dunbar)

Hot dogs are made by placing them in a pan of boiling water, or on a grill, or on a wienie stick, and cooking them. They are especially good when made with mustard, ketchup, and onions.

I got an *F.* Before class was over. She didn't want to know how *I* made hot dogs, she wanted to know how Oscar Meyer and all the others did. She was so moved by my stupidity that she gave me another chance. I didn't waste it. I checked out encyclopedias, read *Consumer Reports,* and called the FDA to see what they had to say about hot dogs. I was so sorry I did. I'd have been happier with the *F.*

Do you know what goes into those things? Do you know what the FDA even allows in them? I'm not talking about what the ingredients label says. It may say beef by-products and you don't think anything about it. But do you know what beef by-products are? Anything that jumps onto the conveyor belt next to beef and sits by it and gets ground up with it— that's a beef by-product. Okay, I'm exaggerating a little. But *only* a little. By the time I got done finding out what was really in hot dogs, I never wanted to eat one again. So I haven't. And that hurt. My research and knowledge had wiped out one of my four basic food groups. For the rest of my teenage life I had to exist on hamburger, chips, and colas. Then she wanted me to research chips. No way!

Next you learn comparison shopping. That's where you price the same item at twenty-five different places to see who's got the best price. At first it's fun going to the mall for "homework." After a while, since you don't get to spend any real money except your own, which isn't very much and doesn't last very long, it becomes like regular homework—boring. You also read *Consumer Reports*. It's a magazine that takes different products, tests and rates them, and then tells you which is the best buy. It's not as much fun as the mall, but your legs aren't nearly as tired when you finish.

By the end of the class you are supposed to be a qualified, deep-thinking, comparison-shopping consumer. That's a good thing. There are lots of companies out there trying to get our money. Think of how many times you've bought something because of an ad (or other stupid reason) and it turned into a consumer fiasco. I remember buying QT Suntanning Lotion—you know "Quick Tanning, without the sun." I have always been a tad pale, even in the middle of summer. I was so pale that I didn't have "bikini line"—I was darker under my suit. So I bought the QT, confident of my soon-to-be-arriving tan. I rushed home, hiding it from my dad, who thought it was the dumbest thing he had ever heard of. Just after I put it on, Dad announced that my goofy orange friend Greg was there to see me. Well, I had always known Greg was goofy, but had never thought of him as orange. But Dad was right. There Greg was, orange all over (or so he said, I took his word on the "all over" part). Guess why? You're right, it's because he had bought QT and put it on himself that morning. It had turned him orange all over. I headed for the shower. Too late. Sometime in the middle of the night my sheets, pajamas, and skin turned bright orange. I could have done color ads for the Florida Citrus Council from my room. I managed okay, though. I never even got embarrassed in front of my friends. Of course, a ski mask does get a little sweaty in July.

If I had been a good consumer I would have taken the time to learn the truth about QT. Maybe you've done something almost as silly. Isn't it nice there's a class that helps save us from ourselves? It can save us money, too.

Wise choices are something we all need to learn to make— and not just with money. Satan is a master of advertising. He shows us pretty things, things we think will make our lives better and more fun. But, like most advertising, he never tells the whole truth. Like getting high might sound—maybe even look—pretty good. Until you're so high you fly your car into a bridge abutment and they have to pry you out with a crowbar. Or you think quick sex, just for fun, could be exciting—and you end up at the VD clinic or pregnant or both.

Consumer Economics teaches us about making wise money choices. It should remind us that we also need to be wise consumers of life. We need to look at what we are purchasing with our lives and what the true costs are. Are we getting what we need—or just what we want? Is what we want the best for us? What's it really going to cost us?

When you're doing product research for Consumer Econ, do a little on your life as well. Make sure you're spending your most valuable resource—*you*—well.

This course includes a study of basic journalistic writing. Students will practice basic journalism techniques, analyze the elements of noteworthy news reporting, and actually produce the school newspapers.

• • • •

Mr. Hinshaw: Newspaper journalism, once thought unlikely to produce superstars, has done so recently. Can anyone name two famous journalists?
Dianne: How about Woodward and Bernstein?
Mr. Hinshaw: Very good—and where in the paper would you find them?
Dianne: On the funny pages.
Mr. Hinshaw: On the funny pages?
Dianne: Sure, Bernstein's the guy who draws that bear family and Woodward is Snoopy's friend.

• • • •

All the news that's unfit to print. That seems to be what's in most school newspapers. Terrible cartoons, lousy editorials, rotten reporting, and worst of all, they always spell *your* name wrong. Every time you pick a copy up you think, *I could do better*. But there comes a time when you've voiced this sentiment once too often. Your friends are sick of hearing about it. To get them off your back, you go and sign up for Journalism. That's when you learn *why* school papers are so bad.

For one thing there are lots of the really smart kids involved in the process. You know the ones I mean—the kids whose hair is always combed perfectly, chinos creased like a razor, Izods without a trace of lint or pillball anywhere, boat shoes fashionably scuffed, and straight As in everything. All the teachers like them, too. They're there because they figure they are going to get the Pulitzer Prize for their articles on sanitary school bathrooms. Their writing is often like them—too

101

squeaky clean to be very likable. Usually they're the ones writing the glowing feature stories profiling the principal and all the teachers. Either that or they write the advice column, "Ask Muffy."

Dear Muffy:
What should a girl do on Saturday night when she doesn't have a date?

Lonely Louise

Dear Louise:
Though I wouldn't really know what to do since Bradway Moneybags, III, and I are always busy, I would suggest that you volunteer your time to a local agency that needs help. It is ever so the right thing to do, heaven knows the poor things (and you, too) need help.

Muffy

Then there are the amateur Ansel Adamses—the photographers. The teacher usually picks a kid who hasn't done anything right since kindergarten, when on the first day of school they asked him for his records and he said he had left them at home with his record player. It's gone downhill for him since. Now all of a sudden, just because he's in Journalism, he is trusted with five thousand dollars worth of camera equipment. And he carries it all with him all the time. A 35mm SLR camera is slung over one shoulder, a viewfinder camera is on the other, a light meter hangs from his neck like some sort of a photographic crucifix, a tripod's strapped to his back, and he has two strobe lights attached to the sides of his head so he's ready to shoot wherever he is, no matter how dark. And he does. Usually at you, when you've just turned on the drinking fountain and sprayed yourself and have water dripping from your nose to your Nikes.

Next, there's the literate type. She's the one who aspires to being the newest of the new poets. She reviews movies (which she calls *films* or *cinema*), books, the art class's latest offerings, and regularly writes poetry for the paper. It's always avant-garde, which is French for "hard to understand." It all sounds like

> *Morning calls out to*
> *Me like a thousand tiny children*
> *On little cats' paws*
> *Saying,*
> *All my life's a circle*

Something like that must really be good because it sure is hard to understand. Everyone else is always saying how deep it is. Either they are a lot smarter than we are (a distinct possibility), or they don't know what it means either and figure it must be deep because it sure is unundsrstandable.

We'd better not forget the sportswriter. The Latin term for sportswriter is *frustratedus jockus*. That's because most school paper sportswriters want to be Varsity in all sports and can't make the JV Tiddlywinks team. Vicariously victorious through the varsity club members' exploits, he records everything about them with a kind of "gee-whiz, good-gosh almighty, weren't they just great last game" attitude that almost makes you nauseous when you read it. It's not so much sportswriting as it is sportsworshiping.

There is also the deep thinker. That's the person who likes to think deep thoughts—or at least they think they think deep thoughts. They think about everything from the meaning of life to why the school food's so crummy. You know why the school food is crummy. It's because it's school food. But the deep thinker sits around thinking deep thoughts about the real reason for the cafeteria consumables' crumminess.

This person is usually the editor, too. In addition to sitting around thinking deep thoughts, his or her main contribution is to write the editorial. The editorial is a chance to share deep thoughts with the whole student body. In print. For time immemorial. So they do. And hardly anybody reads them—except of course, for those who listen to the person in the first place.

Finally, there's you. An average kid. Not too deep, not into sports, not full of advice, but a good kid nonetheless. You get to paste-up the paper, layout the classifieds, and occasionally write a piece on something the deep-thinking editor feels even you, with your limited abilities, might not mess up. And you do quite well, even if it is unrecognized by the rest of the staff.

Sometimes, while pasting-up everybody's stuff into a nice-looking paper, you wonder how, with all the diverse characters working on it, the school paper ever gets out. But, as you learn in Journalism, it's exactly that mixture that *makes* it come out. Everybody has to work together to get it done, even if you can hardly stand one another any other time. You become a team, with each person bringing his or her own strengths to the process. The kid who's always been a nerd isn't one when he's working with his camera. He's finally found his place to excel and comes up with some classic shots of the football team's agony at the missed field goal that cost them the game. The sportswriter sketches the story in with a pen primed with pathos. The editorial is less about deep thinking and more about the support and friendship the team gave the placekicker in spite of the miss. Even the poet has a touching line or two about the whole matter. You get to put it together in a format that looks as good as anything *USA Today* could come up with.

Yes, people of the press are different. But it's a good difference. Just like the world. It would be an awfully boring place if we were all the same. So we're not. God planned it that way. (And the guys at Ford think *they* have a better idea.)

Each of us has strengths. Working together, we can find that we work well. We can get things done we couldn't do by ourselves. We also learn that those we thought different from us aren't really. Sure there are some quirks and patterns and personalities that are not just like ours. But we come to see their worth. In doing so we can find our own.

God certainly made a rainbow of us. What makes a rainbow pretty is how all the colors work together, blending from one to the next. You're part of a rainbow. Journalism may remind you of that.

When you look around, amazed at all the different types it takes to make a paper work, think of all the different types it takes to make life rich and fulfilling. You're one of those parts, you know. That should make *you* feel good.

Required of all tenth grade students. This course is designed to acquaint the student with current health problems. Students consider solutions to contemporary health concerns of personal as well as social nature.

••••

Mrs. Newlin: Today we want to talk about the current health problem that concerns you most. Does anyone have one they would like to ask a question about?

Liz: How about bladder control?

Mrs. Newlin: Well, Liz, I don't know that that's a real issue of contemporary health, but if you would like then—

Liz: You could answer with a hall pass. *Please?!*

••••

Except for the first sentence, which sounds almost as ominous as what the judge says at the end of an old "Perry Mason" show, the rest of the course description sounds like a real snoozer. You know what I mean. This is the kind of course you sign up for and sleep through. An A easier than Beginning Recess.

"Say, Bob, would you mind waking me up if I start snoring."

"Be glad to, because if I don't you're going to have a current health problem—probably shortness of breath."

"Really? Snoring does that?"

"Yeah, because if Mr. Newman catches you he'll strangle you."

"Current health problems"—you already know many of them. Cancer, heart disease, and that other stuff. Your parents are always talking about who's got it now. You know it's not you or your friends. It's old people. People in their thirties and

107

forties. You know all you need to. After all, it's not going to get you anyhow, you're young.

There is good news and bad news. The good news is you are partly right. You *are* young. The bad news is you may be young and still get any or all of the above. There is more good news: You're probably not going to talk much about any of the above stuff anyhow. There's more bad news too: What you are going to talk about is worse. A lot worse. It's personal.

What you're going to talk about are "social diseases." The name "social diseases" makes them sound not-so-bad. In fact, they sound harmless, like something you'd pick up at a church social. You know, a bad tummy ache from eating too much at the ice cream social. Or maybe blisters on your feet from the roller-skating social. Or worse yet, hay caught in your underwear while riding on the Hayride Social. But social diseases are none of these. Social disease is a polite way of saying V.D. Venereal disease. A sexually transmitted disease (STD).

In Health you'll learn all their names. *Syphilis. Gonorrhea. Herpes. AIDS* (which isn't always transmitted sexually, but can be). You'll also learn what they can do to you. You'll see graphic pictures that gross you out. You'll hear stories of what they do. But you might not be paying too much attention. After all, you're a good Christian kid. You go to church and Sunday school and youth group. Christian kids don't have to worry about such diseases. Or do they?

A recent study of the sexual activity of churchgoing teens says that you do. You, as a group, are about as active as your non-churchgoing friends. You know what the church and the Bible say about premarital sex. You know how your parents feel. I'm not going to tell you what you should or shouldn't do. You already know that. The question is—what are you *going* to do? Health class is one place to begin thinking it through.

Besides the emotional and spiritual damage you risk by sleeping around, look at what can happen to your body. That can be pretty scary.

Maybe you've thought about it and are doing what you know to be the right thing. Think then about the others who don't have the convictions you do. Some sleep around with anyone they can. Then they end up sick. What happens to them? How are they treated? Especially someone with AIDS.

The Bible is full of stories about lepers and how they were treated. They were thrown out of their hometowns. They weren't allowed to see their families. They were left to die in a literal and figurative wilderness. Outcasts. Alone.

Who are the modernday lepers? Do you know any? Could they be the STD victims? Those with herpes? How do you treat them? How should you treat them?

STDs are sad, scary things. They can happen to anyone, careful or not, who takes a chance. But once they happen, the people aren't really different than they were before. They may be sick but they still need love and God's good Word. Jesus knew that. He wasn't afraid to talk to or even touch lepers. He knew that loneliness was the hardest part. I suspect that today Jesus would be with those racked with AIDS or STDs—just as He was with the lepers of His day. He knows God loves them too, in spite of themselves.

When you're sitting in health hearing about all these things that will never happen to you (and I pray you've made the choices to ensure they don't), think of those they do happen to. Maybe you and your church can reach out to them. Maybe you can give them a haven from their loneliness. Don't you think Jesus would want you to?

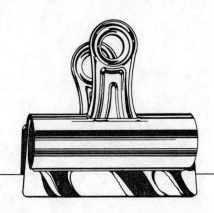

MULLENVILLE SCHOOL DISTRICT
Official Class Schedule

Thomas	John	Alan	11	219
(last)	(first)	(middle)	(grade)	(homeroom)
123 Pleasant Valley Lane		Mullenville	555-5555	488
	(street)	(city)	(phone)	(locker)

Class	Code	Room	Mon.	Tues.	Wed.	Thurs.	Fri.
Drama	e–106	213	X	X	X	X	X
Family Living	he–617	114	X	X	X	X	X
English 11	e–073	320	X	X	X	X	X
Fine Arts Ap	a–461	mus	a–027	X	a–027	X	a–027
Lunch		caf					
Driver's Ed	c–432	lgi	X	s–43	X	s–43	X
Chemistry	s–456	lab	X	X	X	X	X
Study Hall				main auditorium			
Choir	mu–232	mus	X	X	X	X	X

Note: Numbers appearing in weekly schedule indicate study hall seat assignments.

• DRAMA ••

The end result of this course will be a total production involving the entire class. Advanced cuttings from plays will be tried as well as advanced improvisational techniques. Through actual production, all facets of the theater—set design and building, directing, acting, and managing—will be experienced. Students will put together several productions of different types and build a repertoire of material that could be taken various places for performance experience. The course will culminate with the class play.

• • • •

Mr. Morgan: Who can tell me the difference between tragedy and comedy?
Carolyn: Well, comedy is what occurs when my dad first opens my grade card, and tragedy is what follows his closing it.

• • • •

To take Drama or not to take Drama, that is the question. Long before you ever contemplate Hamlet's soliloquy you try to decide whether you're a good enough actor to make an A in class and not get laughed off the stage by your nonthespian friends.

It should be an easy decision. You know you're a natural actor. Miles of home movies made by adoring parents and grandparents (your biggest fans) bear witness to that. "Oh look, Lew, isn't David just the cutest little ham you ever saw? Hit your daddy with the hammer again, you little Valentino." And didn't Miss Turf say you were the best flower in the whole second grade play? Such talent deserves to be shared. More than that, it demands an audience. Watch out Redford and Streep, here you come. Enter, stage right.

So you sign up for Drama. Your parents, the ones who encourage you to be up front every chance you get, know it's because all the talent you have hidden so long is finally working its way to the surface and you'll be a star at last. Your friends think it's only so you can get the lead in the class play (other, less talented kids will have to sing in the chorus), but deep down you know the real reason. You've taken all the proper classes, studied the right stuff to get you into the college of your choice so you'll be able to land some huge-income-producing job with the best company in town. That's all just a safety net. When the local critics see you in the class play, and you are swept along on the shoulders of the adoring audience, everyone will have to admit it would be a shame to waste such talent in Yale Law School. People from Hollywood or Broadway will probably camp out on your front lawn, waiting for the chance to sign you for their newest movie or musical, or just to get your autograph. Your folks will probably even want to sell the house, move to Hollywood, and work as ticket takers at Disneyland just to help you get the start you need.

Then reality sets in—after about the second week of classes: Acting is hard work. What looks so easy on TV, in the movies, or at the theater is difficult and demanding. Lines have to be memorized. Stage directions learned. Rehearse, rehearse, rehearse. You have to learn to live inside a character's life, instead of your own, trying to figure out what makes them do the things the script has them doing. You make mistakes. You stand in the wrong place. Then you blow a cue. You wonder if you'll ever be an actor. But ever so slowly you begin to learn what acting is about and begin to do it pretty well.

We can't all play the lead and we aren't all natural actors. Some of us may never even learn to act. In a play that is. Yet act we do. Every day we play out scenes that, if on film, would impress Siskel and Ebert, the "At the Movies" guys. They've seen it all, good and bad. But they've not seen anything like us. We act happy and carefree, when we really feel as though our lives are falling apart. We act like it doesn't matter that the person we care for most forgot our big date. We do scene after scene, smiling with the friend who just cut us to shreds in front of our other friends, never missing a beat, never showing how we really feel. We do it all perfectly—with never a retake, never a missed cue. Yes, though we may not make it onstage in *Camelot* or *Grease* our bedroom bookshelves could be lined with the Oscars, Emmys, and Tonys won for acting like The Ideally Happy American Teenager—even when we're not.

Acting is a fine art. Good theater commands appreciation. Acting in life, though, is sad. I guess we do it because we think if people saw the real character, the one who is scared, gets hurt, and wants to be loved, they wouldn't like him or her as well as the one we play most of the time—the one who is fearless, untouchable, and self-assured. If they saw the real person behind the Bette Davis eyes, they might turn away.

And they might. That's the scary thing about real life. There is no finished script that binds people to the performance. In a play, they may have to stay and at least act like they like you. In life they don't. Some people won't. No matter what you do, they'll reject you. The more you want them to want you around, the less they will. Unless you act like they want you to, unless you play the part they've written for you in their script.

Jesus knew that. He could have acted like people wanted Him to and everyone would have liked Him. Remember how He rode into Jerusalem on the day we call Palm Sunday and how the people loved Him? The crowd went wild. They laid down their coats in front of Him. They praised God for Him. Why? Because they thought He had come to be their king, to rid them of the revolting Roman rulers. But He hadn't. He told them why He came. He showed them His human side. He cried that week. He got angry. He was scared. And many of the people who had "loved" Him on Sunday, called for His crucifixion on Friday. He wouldn't "act" the way they wanted Him to, so they rejected Him.

Not all of them did. There were those who stood by Him no matter what. John was one. Jesus had shown John His scaredness, loneliness, and uncertainty—and that allowed John to show Jesus his real self, too. They shared a love that we read about today. This love never would have happened if Jesus had "acted" the way most of us "act" today—covering up our feelings.

It's hard to let people in. We might get hurt. But when we do drop the drama and let others come close to us, we find that there are those just like us who are tired of life being a never-ending play and are ready to take the makeup off and be real.

So while you're practicing your part for Drama, stop and think about the acting you do every day. Are you really going for an Academy Award for Best Performance by an Adolescent in a Supporting Role, or do you just want to be you? If it's the latter, remember the One who refused to act the way the people thought a Messiah was supposed to act and continued being Himself. His reward was better than an Oscar, and so will yours be. It's a great thing to be onstage for a little while. It's even better to be able to get off.

May I have the envelope, please?

This course, for both boys and girls, includes a consideration of the student as an individual and his or her relationships to peers and family. Dating, engagement, preparation for marriage, and adjustment to marriage are discussed. Recognition of and dealing with conflicts, as well as avoiding the development of conflicts is covered. Each student develops information into a notebook form on one of the following: wedding or establishment of own apartment. A reception is planned, prepared, and served to guests.

• • • •

Mr. Heald: Let's look at conflict resolution in the family. Jeff, say there's one candy bar and both you and your little sister want it and are almost to come to blows over it. How would you resolve this?

Jeff: Easy, I'd unwrap it and spit on it. Then she wouldn't want it anymore.

• • • •

Family living is one class you usually enjoy. After all, it's about stuff you're interested in, like dating and what comes after dating. No, I don't mean getting home and having your parents want to know what you did on your date. I mean getting married. But for now the main attraction is all the talk about dating.

You figure this class will be a breeze because it's about things you already know. Hey, this is eleventh grade, not kindergarten. You've been on a date before. Maybe even more than one. You're an old pro at this guy/girl thing. What's to learn?

Lots!

Dates can be a lot of fun or they can turn into something that makes *Nightmare on Elm Street* look like a church picnic. You know what I mean. You set up a date. Suddenly you find it's the big night and you're in a car going somewhere with this attractive member of the opposite sex. Since you've been sitting in an awkward silence for what seems like six or seven hours you decide to speak. That's when you find out you don't know what to say. When you finally do, it comes out sounding stupid. Or you look down and find one of your socks is blue and the other one is red, and your shoes don't match either, or your blouse is buttoned up wrong or a big zit just grew instantaneously in the middle of your forehead or any one of a billion other things.

Then there are the bad times, like when you find you're out with someone who is really nerdy and you can't stand. There are even worse times when you're the one who's really nerdy and you're out with someone you want to impress. There's only one thing worse than being out on a bad date. That's not being on any. Or at least that's how it seems when everyone else is at Spacy Macy's House of Burgers and you're baby-sitting little brother.

The hardest part of being on a date is not actually *being* on the date. The hardest part comes long before the shoes are shined, car waxed, and you've consumed two boxes of TicTacs. The hardest part is asking someone out. This used to be an exclusively male horror. But this is the twentieth century. In these days of equal opportunity, a girl can make as big a fool of herself as any guy.

I'll never forget the first time I asked someone out. It was horrible. Years of psychotherapy have not helped. Let me tell you about it—it may help us both.

One of the most beautiful girls I had ever seen moved to our school. She was *one* of the most beautiful because her twin sister was the other. Her name was Sharon Nance. She was in my Spanish class. I had worshiped her from seat 3-A for half a semester. I figured if I was ever gong to get her to go out with me I'd better make a move fast, otherwise one of the hunks or even the nerds would ask her first. Being the smooth operator I was, I knew I'd have no problems, even though it would be my first real date. I had practiced for the big moment by repeating my lines over and over to whichever one of my three little sisters I could con into listening to me. I was ready.

The following is a verbatim account of just how ready I wasn't. The words you are about to read were actually said. They were uttered on March 21, 1968, at 10:57 A.M. in the first floor hallway just outside the southwest auditorium doors at Columbus West High School (I told you I'd never forget).

Scene: The Hallway
Players: Sharon and her friends and Brent and his.
The scene opens with Sharon and her friends standing in a semicircle by the auditorium doors, talking. Brent and his friends come strolling nonchalantly (or trying to) down the hallway. They stop by the girls and try to make eye contact. The girls' talking turns to whispering and giggling.
Brent: Hi, Sharon. What's going on?
Sharon: Oh, nothing, why?
Brent: No reason. Say you wouldn't want to go out with me this weekend, would you?
Sharon: Sure, sounds like fun.
Brent: Well, that's okay. I didn't think you would. (Begins to walk away.)
Sharon: I said *yes*!!
Curtain

That's exactly the way it happened. None of the names have been changed to protect the innocent. It was only one of many reasons I was glad to see Graduation Day come, but it was a big one. Graduation meant I wouldn't have to see Sharon every day and be reminded of how badly I'd blown asking her out. I kept praying she'd forget. By now she probably has. I hope. We haven't seen each other for almost twenty years and if we do I know I'll tell her I'm somebody else and don't have the faintest idea of what's happened to that "silly Brent Bill."

Dating is only one of the things you'll talk about in Family Living. Soon you'll pass it and get into the serious stuff like marriage and having babies of your own. Yes, kids. Yard apes. Rug rats. Driving *you* crazy (and your parents loving every minute of it.) Some teachers have come up with a unique idea to help you experience what it means to be a parent. They give you an egg and tell you to pretend it's your new baby and you have to take care of it night and day for a week. You have to get an egg-sitter if you want to go out. You have to keep it safe from would-be cannibals around the house. You have to act *eggs*actly like a parent. To a point. At the end of the week you can eat your baby if you want. (I know some parents who wish they had had that option with their kids.)

You also learn about conflicts and how to handle them. Conflicts are something we all have to face. It's part of family living—and I don't mean the course. Living together, even with people you love, isn't always easy. But it has its rewards. Home, after all, is the place where they have to take you in whether they like you or not. And most of them do. We take joy in sharing the good times with our families. We find comfort for the sad times.

Family Living can also remind us of another family we have—our Christian family. All around us are people who are part of our family of faith—our brothers and sisters in Christ. Sometimes we don't even know how many other family members there are in school with us. That's sad. If we find out, we can help one another through some of the rough times we all experience at school. Sometimes, though, we're too shy about our faith to let anybody even know we have any.

So, enjoy Family Living—making wedding plans, setting up apartments, and carrying eggs around. Also remember your family of faith. Why don't you look around for the brother or sister in your class right now? You might want to arrange a family reunion.

(e-073)

This course consists of sections on literature and grammar. The literature study covers selections by many American and British authors and includes short fiction, drama, nonfiction, and poetry. Often drawing on themes from the literature section, students will spend time developing advanced composition and research skills.

• • • •

Mrs. Deming: Okay class, now that we have completed our study of poets, I want you to spend some time coming up with a poem in the tradition of the great English poet, Elizabeth Barrett Browning. Take some time and then I'll have you recite them for the class.

Timothy: A Sonnet:

How do I love thee,
Let me count the ways
One, two, three, four. . .

• • • •

Poetry. The art form of love. The stuff made up of rhyme and meter, often without reason. It rolls off the tongue and warms us inside. Actually, to most of us most of it sounds like a bad birthday card—from someone who didn't care to send the very best.

"Okay K mart shoppers, we've got a blue-light special on tacky greeting cards in aisle five."

Usually the worse it is, the more your grandmother likes it. If it all rhymes and sounds like it could send a diabetic into insulin shock, then it's the kind she likes.

"Isn't that a lovely poem? I wish you could write like that."

You're glad you can't.

Some of it is insufferable. Fortunately, in English 11 you won't be studying your grandma's favorite poets. This is one thing you and your teacher agree on. It may be the only thing. At least you are safe from poems by "The Sweet Singer of Michigan" and other neo-schlock poets of the twentieth century. That's the good news.

The bad news is that you start out on classic narrative poetry. That doesn't sound too bad. Narrative poetry could almost be a story. You had stories in English 10. You know you can handle the narrative part. The word that should warn you is *classic*. Classic in literature is not quite like classic in cars, those thirty-five years old or so. Nope. Classic in literature means *real* old, like from centuries ago. That may not seem so bad, but let's look at an example of "classic narrative poetry," *Sir Gawain and the Green Knight.*

The book cover says it's a new verse translation. That doesn't sound too scary. At least it's not in Old English, or whatever it was they spoke back when it was a best-seller. It is also about knights and damsels in distress and that sort of stuff—a kind of medieval *Star Wars.* It may even be interesting.

So you begin to read. It's a little difficult at first, but you make headway. And then you hit passages like

> And then the season of summer with the soft winds
> When Zephyr sighs low over seeds and shoots;
> Glad is the green plant growing abroad,
> When the dew at dawn drops from the leaves,
> To get a gracious glance from the golden sun.

What?

Oh well, it's early in the poem, you think. *Surely, it'll get better.* Or at least understandable. It doesn't. At the end of the classic narrative poem you're wondering what you just read.

But time, and English 11, wait for no one. You advance centuries in only weeks. Soon you're learning about the Puritan poet Anne Bradstreet and later, Ralph Waldo Emerson. You get chills reading "Raven" by Poe and you get cold feet from being "Snow-Bound" with John Greenleaf Whittier. You sing with Walt Whitman

> I celebrate myself, and sing myself,
> And what I assume you shall assume,
> For every atom belonging to me as good belongs to you.

We all find poets and poems that seem to speak to something inside of us. For some it is Emily Dickinson, for others Stephen Crane. Robert Frost talks soothingly about "Stopping by Woods on a Snowy Evening," but then shocks us with the story of a boy killed unexpectedly at suppertime by a buzz saw he's reaching to shut off, concluding with

> No one believed. They listened at his heart.
> Little—less—nothing!—and that ended it.
> No more to build on there. And they, since they
> Were not the one dead, turned to their affairs.

Poetry can lift us—or bring us down.

As we learn from the poets, we see why they have so powerfully spoken to people throughout history. Poetry, done well, speaks lyrically, rhythmically, and forcefully to our inner lives. It resonates with our inner feelings—feelings we often carefully hide from even our closest friends. Feelings that at times we are unsure of.

There is much great poetry in the Bible. Pick up the Psalms and hear their humanness. They run the gamut of human emotions—joy and despair, worship and disbelief. The writers knew how they felt and they knew how to write it so that you would feel it too. Their words speak to everyone who follows.

The God whom they address hears their hearts as well. He is no spirit sitting somewhere in space unconcerned for us tiny humans. Though at times seeming distant, God cares when those who love Him express themselves through the beauty of poetry. God sees all those feelings, whether they are happy, sad, glad, or mad. God hears and responds.

When you are tempted to give up on poetry—look at it again. Let the words flow over your soul. And maybe, just maybe, you'll feel like a poet and want to write something of your own to the One who inspired all poets. I'm sure it would be appreciated.

This course is designed for the college-bound student who needs a general knowledge of art, music, dance, and drama. Special emphasis will be given aesthetic appreciation and application to everyday life. Course outline will include several field trips to the local symphony, ballet, theater, and museum of art as well as basic historical knowledge. Musical and/or artistic ability not required.

• • • •

Mr. Chilcoat: Now, who here can answer the following question? What do you know about Liszt?
Sharon: I know a lot, I know a lot!
Mr. Chilcoat: All right, Sharon. Tell us about Liszt.
Sharon: Well, every night before I go to bed I make a liszt of everything I have to do the next day.

• • • •

In appreciation courses you really don't have to have any artistic or musical ability. Unless, of course, you consider knowing how to put on a set of headphones or watch slides artistic ability. That's the really nice thing about this course. You don't have to be able to paint well or sing on key. The only ability you'll need is to be able to stay awake when the teacher turns the lights out and starts showing slides. Believe me, you'll need it.

"This slide is a detail of the right side of El Greco's famous 'Burial of Count Orgaz.' Please notice how the monk's sleeve is about to catch fire from the torch being held by the young man with the frilly collar. The next slide is a detail of the same painting, but of the left side. Notice the fine detailing of the priest's surplice. This next slide is a detail of the center, which shows Jesus in heaven, looking down on all this. The following slide is a detail of. . ."

129

This is usually all after lunch too, so you're ready for a good nap. A darkened room, softly humming projector, and monotonic teacher does not help defeat drowsiness during the "visual presentation of the Dutch Masters' best work." By the way, these are not the guys who make cigars—these are the artists from seventeenth-century Holland.

The art appreciation part can be tedious. The music part can be worse. In order to expose you to the musical classics (*classics*—there's that word again. Drawing on your experience from English 11, try to remember why that would be a warning signal), you'll be instructed in the fine art of putting on headphones. Up to this point it's a lot like language lab. Then you'll listen to the works of the great composers. That's not Billy Joel, John Cougar Mellencamp, or Bruce Springsteen, either. You'll hear the B-Boys. No, not the Beach Boys, the *B-Boys*—Bach, Beethoven, and Brahms. At first it sounds like the supermarket music your folks play in the car on the way to Grandmother's house for dinner. You know the stuff I mean. "WZZZ—the sound of eaazzy listening." If it got any easier you wouldn't have to listen at all, which doesn't sound like a bad idea after the four-hour trip to Grandma's.

The thing about classical, though, is it's not all bland like supermarket music. Just when you're getting good and comfy, ready to soar off into snoozeland in a soothing, symphonically induced sleep, somebody bangs on a timpani and brings in the brass section. Scares you to death. After all, you were almost asleep. Mozart and his friends were no fools. They knew how to make an audience sit up just when it got a little too cozy. And they did it without million-watt amps and electric guitars and pianos.

The best thing about the class is the field trips. They are fun. Except for the part about getting all dressed up and having to put on one of your father's neckties so you can get into the theater. I remember going to the Ohio State University Drama Department's production of Shakespeare's *The Tempest*. The idea of Shakespeare didn't thrill me—I was a typical junior—but the thought of cruising the campus at night with my friends did. So I went. Besides, I needed the grade. We were used to special effects in movies and were interested in how they were going to make someone suddenly appear on stage, as it said in the book. We knew how they did it in movies—they simply stop the camera, have the person take their mark, and restart the scene. Presto! One minute no one's there, the next the Alien Ax Murderer from Planet Blood appears. We just couldn't imagine how they would do it live on stage.

> "Okay everybody, there's a special effect coming. When I shout, 'Shut,' then shut your eyes and when I yell, 'Open,' open them."

Nope, just wouldn't work.

What they did worked. When it came time for the sprite (no, not the soft drink, a real sprite, like Tinkerbell) to appear, somebody offstage set off a cannon containing a blank shell. We thought the Russians had dropped the big one. I was sure it was World War III, and I had forgotten where the fallout shelter was. When I finally got my heart beating again, there was the sprite, on stage, ready to say her lines.

It worked. I was impressed. And not just with the special effects. Some by my girl friend's fingernails, which were deeply imbedded in my palm, thanks to the cannon shot. They were still there years later when we got married.

We see art, hear music, and watch drama every day. Often we don't realize or appreciate the effort that must happen to make a piece work. We need to. True, much of what we see would not be considered fine art. But fine art often turns up in the craziest places. Listen to the background score of a Bugs Bunny or Mickey Mouse cartoon. If you've paid attention in music appreciation, you'll probably recognize some of those musical themes. Many of them are orchestral classics. Almost every week on TV there's a modern day remake of *Romeo and Juliet*—an old, but ever-young love story.

Even popular entertainment at its hokiest borrows from the fine. The old TV sitcom "Green Acres" is an example. When

Lisa (Eva Gabor) and Oliver Wendell Douglas (Eddie Albert) pose with a pitchfork at the close of the opening credits they're doing a parody of Grant Wood's painting, *American Gothic*. It's a case of television life imitating art, imitating life.

There is a lot around us that is really fine. We need to learn to appreciate it. God has given us many good things, things that help make our lives beautiful—music, art, drama. And though at times all classical seems to sound the same (just like rock and roll does to our folks), we can be thankful for it and see how it enriches all of us. It even stretches our tastes to allow more of God's goodness in.

Much of good music, art, and drama has been dedicated to God's glory. Handel's *Messiah* and Michelangelo's *Pieta* are just two examples. They are attempts to express an appreciation of beauty to the One who created all of art.

Maybe the next time you're sitting in class bleary eyed, listening to the "Bradenburg Concerto" for what seems like the fifty-fifth time that hour, you'll want to really listen. You just might even want to take some time to get a little closer to the One who inspired the sounds sifting through the stereo. That same Singer will help you appreciate the beauty that's been created for your enjoyment.

(c-432)

In addition to classroom training in the operation of motor vehicles and state and federal laws governing their use, the student will have actual hands-on experience in driving an automobile. Successful completion of this course is generally recognized by most insurance companies as a good reason for lower rates for young people.

• • • •

Mr. Thornburg: Today we are going to go for our first ride. Is everybody buckled in? Good. Now, Nancy, first move the gear selector to D for Drive. Very good. Now check the street for oncoming traffic, then when the road is clear, gently depress the accelerator and pull out of our space and drive down the street. Well, that wasn't too bad. Now, Nancy, put the gear selector in R for Reverse, look behind you to check traffic, and carefully back out of Mrs. Clark's living room. Sorry about your TV set, Mrs. Clark. See you again soon, I'll bet.

• • • •

Ah, Driver's Ed. The thrill of the open road. The swish of the tires on the thruway. The roar of the wind through open windows as you cruise effortlessly at fifty-five miles per hour. The screams of the Driver's Ed teacher whenever you make a sudden move.

To be truthful, not many of them scream. Most of them just sit there, calm as can be. They have all the nervous energy of Don Johnson on tranquilizers. It makes you wonder where they get Driver's Ed instructors, doesn't it? They all appear to have nerves of steel. They act like they've seen it all before. That's because they have. There is nothing you can do to them that someone else hasn't already done. Or they haven't done to themselves. If you promise not to tell where you learned this (it is classified information, after all), I'll tell you where they get these teachers.

134

Every year the school administrators go down to the Bureau of Public Records. There they look for the teachers who had the worst driving records as teenagers. To qualify, there must be a separate computer containing your records only. You must average an accident or speeding ticket every fifteen minutes from the time you got your learner's permit until you turned twenty-one. You don't believe me? Read on.

The best example I know of is a friend of mine who was once (and may yet be if he's still alive) a Driver's Education teacher. I'll change his name so that if any of you get him you won't be afraid to get in the car with him. We'll just call him Mr. Rogers. (Can *you* say Mr. Rogers? I *like* the way you say that.)

Everything I'm going to tell you is true. Court records back it up. And I'm not going to tell you everything that I could. You don't want to know *everything*.

To say that Mr. Rogers was a reckless driver as a kid would be a lot like saying that Adolf Hitler might have done some bad things. Mr. Rogers, as a youth, helped rewrite Ohio's driving laws. New legislation was passed almost daily just to try to keep him under control on the county roads. The cities were left to defend themselves.

Mr. Rogers' cars always looked as if he had just competed in the Fayette County Fair Demolition Derby. They looked that way *before* he got to the fair. He never even competed in a demolition derby. Mr. Rogers got his dents the hard way—he earned them. He once drove off a hill in his car. Not over—*off*. That was one of the less scary experiences.

The worst happened when he was out driving one evening and as usual going a little faster than he should have. Not much, just thirty to fifty miles or so over the limit. There was a curve in the road he should have remembered. He didn't. Just outside the curve was a house he shouldn't have driven through. He did. He went straight when the road went left and gave the house a drive-in living room. It might not have been so bad except there was a witness. The lady who lived there saw it all. Though I've told you what happened, she had a whole other perspective on the situation. I couldn't begin to explain the surprise she must have felt watching her home disintegrate and having a car stop a foot or so from the sofa on which she was sitting. I'm not sure she could either. In the sheriff's report she comes across as a master of understatement.

"Well, I was sittin' dere watchin' TV whens all of a sudden dere was dis Ford coming at me."

I know Sony claims their picture is lifelike, but that's not the kind of lifelike she wanted when she bought the set. Mr. Rogers had come right through the wall where the TV was and stopped right in front of her. It makes the Duke Boys' driving look wimpy, doesn't it? The thing you need to keep in mind is that this guy is now teaching people like you how to drive.

So now you know why Driver's Ed teachers don't seem nervous. How nervous would you be if you had totaled six cars, three houses, and fourteen telephone poles by the time you were seventeen? What would there be to be nervous about? What could a student driver do to you that you hadn't already done to yourself?

Driver's Ed is exciting. At first it's scary. You see your folks and friends tooling down the road, barely paying attention, with their wrist draped loosely over the wheel. It looks so easy. So effortless. Then it's your turn. When you're first starting out, every time you sneeze you change three lanes. You ease down slowly on the accelerator and suddenly everything that's not fastened down (including the instructor) is in the trunk. How could something that looks so easy be so hard? Finally you reach the point where you're not scaring all the other people in the car and they don't scare you as much either. You start to feel really good about what you've learned to do. You have turned a ton and a half of potentially dangerous metal, capable of careening around corners and sending people diving for safety, into a tool for you to use to get from one place to the next, safely, efficiently, and comfortably. The uncontrollable has been controlled. The untamed, tamed.

You are now able to take people places. Safely. You can do something that takes a lot of skill and responsibility very well. That feels neat. You've harnessed it to your benefit.

Of course it takes a while to learn that. You have to learn all the laws of your state. You have to come to know just what a car will and will not do. How it goes. Stops. Turns. What it can be depended on to do if you want it to. And what it won't do, no matter how much you want it to. You have to learn how to steer, stop, and go, and keep doing all of it until it becomes almost automatic. You have to look at highway safety movies, the kind that usually feature someone who tried to make a car do what it couldn't or forgot their own limitations, and ended up looking like 140 pounds of ground beef. Driving is an immense privilege and joy, and an awesome responsibility.

Taking time alone with God is a lot like Driver's Ed. Knowing how a car works, what it will and won't do, helps us cruise safely without endangering ourselves or others. Time alone with God, talking about our feelings, allows us to enjoy life. Being a teenager can be a lot of fun, but it can be dangerous too. Look at all the kids who have cracked up on the freeway of life, broken by drugs and alcohol, unwanted pregnancies, trouble with the law, and so on. All because they couldn't control the most intricate machine of all—their emotions.

Life can be a ball, or hell. Quiet time with God can give us the help we need to enjoy life responsibly. God made us. He knows what makes us work. He knows our feelings can control us if we don't learn to control them. It's not easy. Just like a turbocharged Thunderbird, feelings can get out of control easily if we're not sure how to use them.

Think of what the streets, roads, and highways around your town would be like with untrained drivers in unguided metal missiles zipping down the streets. Fun for some, scary for most, and dangerous for all. There would be accidents all over the place. Learning to control the Chevy is necessary for us to get around safely.

Learning to talk to God about what we are feeling—about anything—doesn't hinder our progress toward where we are going. It actually helps us get there in one piece, if we just listen. God wants us to get through life safely. He made us and knows what's best. Time with God is not meant to be restrictive but liberating. It allows us to be us safely, enjoying life as God wants us to.

As you buckle on your Bell safety helmet, about to climb into the Driver's Ed Dodge, thank God for the safety of sane, educated drivers. And for the safety taking time with Him brings, too.

(s-456)

Chemistry is a course designed to meet the needs of college-bound students. Several principles and fundamental chemical concepts are studied, including: the classifications of matter and their changes, atomic and molecular structure, periodicity of the properties of the elements, the naming of inorganic compounds, bonding in compounds, and chemical equations. Also studied are physical and chemical properties of solids, liquids, and gases, the gas laws, acid and base theories, and various types of equilibrium.

• • • •

Chris: Mr. Pierson, Scott wants to know what happens when you mix H_2O, silver nitrate, and U-235 isotope in a glass flask and heat it over a Bunsen burner?
Mr. Pierson: Well, Chris, I'm not sure. But that sounds really dangerous. You send him over right now and have him ask that silly question himself.
Chris: Well, I've got a feeling he'd really like to, but he already did his experiment and we can't quite find him just now.

• • • •

Chemistry is the last of the basic science courses to be taken. That is, if you really want to take one more science course. It is the final step in the acquisition of scientific knowledge. In language you'd understand—after this you don't have to take any more science.

Mr. Webster, and his faithful sidekick, Dictionary, have this to say about chemistry— "I don't want to take it!!" Oops, excuse me, my mistake, that's what the junior class said. What Webster said is this, chemistry is "the science dealing with the composition and properties of substances, and with the reactions by which substances are produced from or converted into other substances."

You understand that, don't you? Good. Would you please

explain it to me? I think it means that you'll learn how things are put together and ways to put other things together from the things you have that are already put together. That's much simpler, don't you agree?

Chemistry sounds like it could be the most fun science class so far. Don't be fooled. Chemistry is not what you have been led to believe. It has nothing to do with the nifty chemistry kits your older brother got for Christmas when you were young. You're not going to invent invisible ink and make purple clouds appear over the lab or build baking soda volcanoes that erupt or any other neat stuff like that. Just like English 11 poetry is different from what Grandma reads, so too is high school chemistry different from Christmas chemistry sets she gave your brother.

What it is about are formulas like

$$\frac{[H+][CN-]}{[HCN]} = \frac{[H+](0.46)}{0.54} = 4 \times 10^{-10}$$

and other things the mortal high school mind can not comprehend. You will not create life (at least, not on purpose) in chemistry class. You will not turn tinfoil into pure gold. Much of the time you will think you're in another math class. If you thought the formulas in algebra were bad, you were right. But chemistry class formulas are worse.

Yes, my friend, the sciences look like fun, but halfway through the first grading period you'll wonder why you're there at all. Then, like Nicolaus Copernicus's discovery that the planets revolved around the sun, it comes to you—it's a required course.

In spite of that you still have to watch out. You just may learn something. After all, the sciences tell us about God's creation. Chemistry, as hard to understand as it is, reveals the intricate complexity of our world and our lives. Biology, which you mastered in ninth grade, may show us the big picture, but chemistry shows us all the little ones that make up the big one. It tells us about atoms and compounds and DNA and all the things that hold our lives together.

Like chemistry, God is complex. We think we know all

there is to know about God. That may be a lot. We may know Him as Parent. Forgiver. Lover. Judge. There's still more. He is all-wise, all-powerful, and everywhere at the same time. Just like chemistry is often more than our minds can comprehend, so too is God. We may think we have Him all wrapped up in nice neat little compartments, but He won't stay there. He breaks out of them. Far too often we make our God too little.

Maybe that makes God manageable in our minds. But it also limits Him—and us. We need to be glad God is complex and bigger than us. Because then we can let Him take care of us, instead of us always having to take care of ourselves. That's a good feeling.

While you're struggling with chemistry, you may want to struggle with God as well. At least with your ideas about who God is and what He's like. Take a new look at this One whom you go to worship each Sunday. As you learn each little piece of chemistry that helps you understand the world, perhaps you will learn a little more about God, too. With understanding comes added help for daily living. Even surviving chemistry.

• CONCERT CHOIR ••

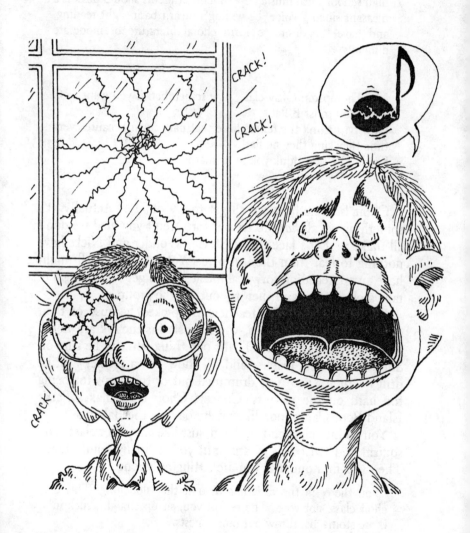

Concert Choir is the large major performing group in the high school vocal music department. Students should possess a pleasant singing voice, be willing to learn basic sight reading, and have the desire to learn choral literature of moderate difficulty.

• • • •

Mr. Thompson: Okay class, now remember, if you want to C sharp you must B flat.
Christy: I think the tenors have that part down because every time they sing they be flat.
Keith: Oh, you think you're so sharp.

• • • •

Choir is something we all get to try out for. Actually, it's something we all *have* to try out for. Aren't you glad we don't all make it? Let's face it, the Stevies Wonder and Nicks have nothing to fear from the rest of us. Yet, so that we all might have an appreciation for vocal music, we all get (okay, *have*) to take a choir class and then try out for the group.

Just like Driver's Ed teachers are picked because of their dangerous driving records, vocal music instructors are nominated for their nastiness. That's one thing you can be sure of. Show me a vocal teacher and I'll show you a former Marine drill instructor who was drummed out of the corps for being too hard on the recruits. Concert Choir class makes Parris Island Boot Camp look like ninety days in the Bahamas.

You go into class and sit down, just like any other class. You squirm and twist and gyrate until you're finally comfortable. Then you find out that you are sitting all wrong.

"You there, in the fiftieth row, quit that slouching. This is choir class, not yoga. The rest of you, sit up straight, suck in those stomachs, throw out those chests."

Most of us throw out our backs trying to follow the directions. As far as the teacher is concerned, we're still sitting

144

wrong. I remember my choir teacher. I'll call her Miss Fawley, mainly because that was her name. Though she was young and attractive, after a couple of weeks in her class we all quit wondering why she wasn't dating anyone. Who would want to go out with her? The woman had crazy ideas about all kinds of things concerning human anatomy and how it was supposed to fit into a chair. According to her, the only part of our bodies that was to touch any part of a chair was about a two-inch strip across our young bottoms. The bottoms of our thighs couldn't. Our backs did not touch the backs of chairs—in her opinion, chair backs were a stupid addition by a demented seating engineer. A date with her would probably have been torture.

"You there, sitting next to me. Sit up straight. There, that's better."

Imagine enduring that throughout dinner and the movies. Three days of choir had me more sore than the twenty-five games of dodge ball in Phys Ed. I asked if I could bring in my dad's La-Z-Boy recliner. Then I got to sit in the hall and think about why that was a stupid idea. I agree it was, but at least I got to rest my back against the wall.

After learning how to sit, comes learning how to breathe. (And you thought you knew this stuff from the time you were born. Fooled you.) You not only have to sit funny in choir, you have to breathe funny, too. The only other place you learn such ridiculous breathing techniques is when you are married, going to have a baby, and go to natural childbirth classes. It's better than choir though, because while you're learning them, you get to do them lying on the floor.

Finally, you begin to sing. After a period of trying different parts, during which time the whole group sounds very similar to a bunch of cats being tortured, the choir is sorted into its various voices—altos, sopranos, tenors, basses, and what's left. The "what's left" kids are usually urged to just lip sync to what the rest of the group's singing so as not to throw everybody else too far off. That's because everybody knows that the kids who sing the worst also sing the loudest. Everybody else sings in a whisper. After all, we don't want to make a mistake. Not because that could upset the teacher. No, we don't mind upsetting her. It's because it would embarrass us in front of our friends.

Then, after months of hard work, what sounded like a cat fight sounds closer to what the composer meant it to. Altos are actually altoing. Tenors need no longer sing "ten-or" eleven miles away. Sopranos have learned the high parts, and the basses are down in the vocal basement. You begin to get a good feeling about having a part in creating something beautiful. It's so personal. It sounds good.

Sometimes going to church is like choir class. Some days we go and sit and squirm. We wonder if our part is ever going to sound right. We get together and screech and howl and make joyful and not-so-joyful noises. At times everyone seems to be a soloist. Everybody with a different song, but all singing at the same time.

The church should be like a choir that has learned and practiced together. Every song should fit, with every singer having a part. It's not a place for superstars. It's to be a place where people work together. If we learn together, under our Director, it will come out like it should. We need to learn to do that—all of us different singers in God's choir. And when we do so, we really do make beautiful music. I'm sure the world is ready to hear some people in harmony. Won't you sing along with the rest of God's choir?

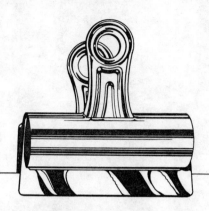

MULLENVILLE SCHOOL DISTRICT
Official Class Schedule

Thomas	John	Alan	12	318
(last)	(first)	(middle)	(grade)	(homeroom)
123 Pleasant Valley Lane		Mullenville	555-5555	1470
(street)		(city)	(phone)	(locker)

Class	Code	Room	Mon.	Tues.	Wed.	Thurs.	Fri.
Home Ec	he–611	117	X	a–134	X	a–134	X
SAT/PSAT	ss–109	352	X	X	X	X	X
Speech	e–107	127	X	X	X	X	X
Accounting	b–550	212	X	X	X	X	X
Lunch		caf					
Comp Gov't	h–255	225	X	X	X	X	X
Comput Science	m–360	104	X	X	X	X	X
English 12	e–096	352	X	X	X	X	X

Note: Numbers appearing in weekly schedule indicate study hall seat assignments.

(he-611)

Practical projects comprise a major portion of this course's work. Basic projects include sewing, personality development, food selection and preparation, the four food groups, and textiles. Cooking is taught from the consumer standpoint as well as the nutritional point of view.

• • • •

Miss Nicholson: Class, today we're going to learn to make white sauce. Now, sauces are very difficult, so watch your recipe very closely. Follow it exactly. Make sure of all your ingredients and measurements. Are there any questions before we start?
Diana: What are we going to do with all the white sauce we make?
Miss Nicholson: Well, the shop class is putting an addition on the building and they ran out of cement. I volunteered our class's help. Any other questions?

• • • •

Home Economics. Sounds like it should be about buying stuff for the house, doesn't it? Sort of a domesticated Consumer Economics. Of course, we all know it's not. It's about baking, and sewing, and all the other stuff people do around the house to keep it going. The school can't call it "Learning How to Bake, Sew, and Do Stuff Around the House," though. If they did, no one would come. So, like the other courses you have to take, whether you want to or not, the school board came up with a name that they hope will make the class sound not too boring.

I now admit that when I was in school I didn't take Home Ec. I wanted to (more than Shop anyhow), but in the olden days of the early sixties guys didn't take Home Ec. Not only did we not take it, we weren't allowed to. Home Economics was for girls. So guys my age never took a class where we got to take bolts of cloth or sacks of raw ingredients and ruin them.

We had to do it all on our own. Today though, in this era of equal opportunity, guys can go to Home Economics and ruin stuff with the girls. Isn't America a great place?

Since we guys didn't get to take it, Home Ec was a mysterious world. We had no idea what was going on behind those closed doors of room 117. The only time I remember having even a glimpse into the wonderful world of women in Home Ec was the day I ripped the seat of my pants. Tight pants were the thing to be wearing and one day after goofing off with my friend Greg, I suddenly found mine so tight that my underwear wasn't under any where. Extreme embarrassment. I heard the "RRRRRIPPPPPP" and, without even a good-bye to Greg, headed for the little boys' room. I figured I would just wait there until dark, by which time everybody would have left the building and I could sneak home. All of my friends, being the kind and sensitive guys they were, decided they didn't want to be seen with me either and left for class. There I was— stranded, alone, and a mile and a half from home—with a distinct breeze filtering through my BVDs. The seconds began to tick away. Three hours later, or so it seemed, ten seconds had passed. It was now 9:01:01. Only six more hours to go till school let out. Only ten till darkness fell. Another three hours passed. Now it was 9:01:21. I couldn't take it. I thought I'd make a break for it. I carefully cracked the door open and glanced out. The coast was clear. Risking the wrath of The Hall Monitor, I was heading for home and new Levis when *she* came around the corner. I was at the point of no return—a mile and half from home and three miles from the boys' bathroom. Nowhere to go. She saw I was in trouble—I think the way I put both my hands over my behind and was scooting along the lockers lining the wall tipped her off. She was a caring kid. She didn't even snicker. And she was headed to Home Ec. I explained my predicament, which was already apparent to her. She volunteered to take my pants into class and do emergency surgery on them. I scooted back to the bathroom, peeled off the jeans, and handed them out the door. Ten minutes later she was back. A knock came on the door and she pushed it gently open, depositing my pants in a pile on the floor. *Ahh, safe at last.* It was then I found out that most girls are about as good at Home Ec as most guys are at Shop.

The pants were sewn—she hadn't let me down there. But not very straight. And the thread showed through on the outside. That wouldn't have been so bad, except that the jeans were blue and thread was pink. While I was no longer going to die from embarrassment, I was severely wounded. The white flag of my undies would have been fatal, the pink thread was not. Still, I heard about it all day—from those same kind and sensitive friends who, if it were up to them, would have me still hiding in the bathroom.

Home Ec is a wonderful thing though, even if that girl did mess up my pants. (The older I get, the more I wonder if she didn't do it on purpose.) You do learn to take raw ingredients and make them into something useful. Bolts of cloth become dresses for the mid-winter prom. Eggs, flour, milk, sugar, and so on are turned into cookies and other foodstuffs. Some of them are even edible. All of it made from materials that are all around us. While humans have made some of them, like the bolts of cloth, even those have to be made from something else. The basic stuff put there by God.

You need to remember that when you're working away in Home Ec. All of it had to come from somewhere and be put there by someone. Home Ec can remind us that we are watched over by a loving and kind God who has put within reach everything that we need to make our lives worthwhile. We have the sun to warm us. We have friends to share our happy and sad days. Most of us have too much food to eat. Many of us have parents who love us deeply. We all have a God who cares more for us than we do for ourselves. Even if that's hard to believe.

Just like Home Ec teaches how to take a recipe and raw ingredients and turn out a scrumptious soufflé, so too do we need to learn to take the raw ingredients of living, put there by God, and turn them into a lovely life. We can you know. All we have to do is sign up for Life Ec and follow the Master Chef's directions. It's one course that's not required—but should be.

For grades 11-12:

This course will be offered the first semester. Students who wish to review techniques for mastering verbal and mathematic skill areas of these tests and to practice simulated test-taking may elect to take this course.

• • • •

Mr. Garris: It is now time to practice test-taking. Though this is only a simulation, this is how the real college board tests are given. Those of you who live through the next three hours may be qualified to pass real tests. As for the rest of you, don't worry, we'll notify the next of kin. Pick up your #2 pencil and begin.

• • • •

I don't know about you but I really looked forward to the SAT test. But then I've always been considered a little strange. There were a couple a good reasons I was ready for it, though. One was that it got me out of class. For the kind of student I was, this was a valid reason. I figured that if I hurried my way through it, I'd have lots of time left over to stare out the window and daydream about girls and cars—the two most unobtainable things in my life. Another reason was that if I got good scores on my tests, they might offset the bad grades I had on my report card—good grades being the other unobtainable thing in my life. This would have the side benefit of getting my dad off my back, too. Since he weighed 165 pounds, that in itself made it worth the effort.

SAT day came. We test-takers—some full of fear (if we got bad grades we didn't get into Harvard), some hopeful (if we got good grades we didn't have to go in the Army)—filed into the library, took our seats, picked up our pencils, and began silently marking computer sheets for the next three hours. It was rough. I wasn't prepared for how tough it would be. I didn't get to think about either girls or cars the whole time. Verbal skills questions came at me from one direction, while math problems zoomed by me at lightspeed the other way. Finally the time was up. It was over. All I had to do now was wait by the mailbox for the scores. Would they be good? Or bad? Would they show that I had the potential my father said (and prayed) I had? Or was I as dumb as a box of rocks? At last they came. The waiting was over. Good news, they were great. I was smarter than any of my teachers suspected. I guess I had fooled them good. I had even fooled myself. Somehow I had learned a lot of things in spite of myself. It looked as though I'd make it into college after all. And I did it all on my own. Back then there was no SAT/PSAT Skills Review Course.

Now there is. Although it hardly seems fair, you're lucky. You can learn the ins and outs, the thou shalts and thou shalt nots of big-time test-taking. You find out when to skip a question and come back to it and when to just keep going. You see questions phrased like those on the real test. All of this helps get you ready for one of the longest three-hour periods of your life. It helps ensure you won't try to stick your head in one of the Home Ec room ovens when you come across a question like

Point (-2,6) is the center of a circle which is tangent to the Y axis. The coordinates of the point of tangency are

a.(-2,0) b.(0,4) c.(-2,-6), d.(0,-2) e.(6,0)

(I had a friend who did that when we took the SAT. It was really sad—turned out it was an electric oven, not a gas one. He felt really dumb later, but he had a great tan.) Knowing what to expect is nice. If you know what's coming, you won't worry nearly so much. It won't all be new and unknown.

A class like this also teaches you how to pace yourself so you'll survive to the end of the test. The way these tests are put together, that's not always easy. A course on testing teaches you that tests are testing. They are. They wipe you out. After our SAT test fourteen kids were admitted to Mount Carmel Hospital for exhaustion. Most were back in class by the end of the year, though, so don't worry too much.

It's really too bad there isn't a course on Life Skills Testing Review. There are many times when life is a lot harder than the SAT test. It doesn't matter how much you study, with life you never even know what question is coming up next. One day it'll be whether to sneak into a movie your parents don't want you to see, but your friends do. The next it may be about going parking or getting drunk. Then there are all the questions about having sex. They always seem to come when we're not ready for them, too. Since we're not, the answer we put down may not be the right one. Usually we don't have to wait for the computer to send back the test results to know whether or not we got a good score. The answer is apparent right away.

Though there isn't a formal course on Life Skills Testing Review, there are some places we can go for help. As hard to believe as it may be, your folks might be useful here. They were teenagers once, you know. They even lived to tell about it. And they faced some of the same problems and decisions you're facing. Sometimes they made the right choice, sometimes the wrong one. If you ask, I'll bet they'd be glad to talk to you about it. That is after they came out of your-asking-them-to-help-induced shock.

Friends can be helpful, too—but only those you know will give you honest answers, not just the ones they think you want to hear. Check out how your Christian friends feel about life and the hard choices you and they have to make.

Whatever you do, don't forget to check with God. God'll talk to you, deep in your heart, if you'll stop long enough to listen. Remember listening to God? We talked about that earlier.

SATs and other tests like it are important. But even more important are the tests you face every day. Just like in

SAT/PSAT Skills Review, you might start reviewing some of the questions you know are going to come up in your life. You'll find it's a lot easier to think of the correct answer now than on test day.

"Time! Put your pencils down and turn your test booklets facedown. Thank you."

(e-107)

This course provides the student with an opportunity to become familiar with a variety of speech-related activities and with speech and drama performance. The four units covered in Speech are: public speaking, debate, oral interpretation, and dramatic interpretation (acting). Included in the public-speaking unit will be the essentials of outlining, constructing, and delivering different types of speeches.

• • • •

Mr. Shields: Can anyone here tell me what they regard as the most important type of speech and why?
Evan: The after-dinner speech, because at least you don't go to sleep hungry.

• • • •

Most of us like to talk. And we do—on and on and on and on. So why is it that when we take a Speech class we're terrified? Our palms get sweaty, our knees shaky, and where our brain used to be we find a note that says, "Decided to move to the Coast. Will write if I get work." Our religious life takes a turn for the better though, as we pray for the school to burn down before we have to get up in front of the class and—and what? Talk. That's all. Something we do all the time and don't even think about.

In Speech class we do. I suppose one reason is that in Speech class there are those nasty things called grades. You're going to get marks on how well you talk.

"Larry, generally your speech was very fine. You had good illustrations, it was evident you outlined the subject, and you knew your material. On that basis I'd give you an *A*. However, since you inserted "y'know" after every third word you get an *F−*."

159

Yes, in Speech class, all the little quirks in your speech patterns (which your parents have been pointing out to you for the last five years) suddenly become evident to you and the entire student body. Sometimes it's embarrassing. In fact, it's always embarrassing. But it's worth it to be able to command people's attention whenever you get up to say something. Yes, it's a high price to pay, but to be an effective, y'know, communicator, you've got to, y'know, learn how to talk good, y'know? I mean, *well*, y'know? Get rid of all that extra stuff, y'know?

That's not always easy. You start out with something speech teachers call "oral interpretation." That's what your second-grade teacher used to call "reading out loud." In oral interpretation you're given something to read— "with feeling. Make the words come alive." Usually it's something supersickening; a subject you couldn't care less about. You get up in front of the class and read. There are times you get into it. After all, some other fool wrote the words, not you. You're just repeating them. What's to be nervous about? After a while, you get fairly comfortable about doing this. That's when the teacher changes the rules.

No more oral interpretation, now it's real speeches. You've got to make up things to talk about. Nothing is going to be handed to you anymore. In the beginning you get to prepare. You learn how to do speech outlines and so on. You get to take them with you when you make your speech. And the speech is only two minutes or so long. Sometimes you even get to pick the topic. All of a sudden, you wish you were back in dumb old oral interpretation. But it's too late. You're now standing in front of the class. They are all staring at you. *Why*, you wonder, *why*? Because it's your turn to speak, that's why.

You start slowly, gaze fixed firmly on the clock at the back of the room, carefully avoiding looking at anyone—especially your friends or the teacher—in the eyes. The second hand moves as slowly as if someone had saturated it with syrup. About halfway through the speech you begin to feel easier, building a little confidence. Then a thought crosses your mind: *Are my pants zipped up?* What do you do? Do you break your cadence by taking your eyes off the script to look at your pants or do you just keep going, hoping no one will notice and you can make it back to your seat and zip them up there? Maybe they're not unzipped. Yeah, that's it. Then you feel a breeze where no breeze should be and you know that the whole class hasn't heard a word you've been saying because they've been too busy staring at your unzipped zipper.

Of course, when you sit down, you find out your pants were zipped and the breeze was your mind going bonkers from all the pressure. What a relief. Actually, it's more than a relief, because the teacher liked the talk and gave you an A. The comfort zone looms again. You begin to relax. That alone should set warning bells clanging. Because now it is time for extemporaneous speeches.

Extemporaneous speeches are the kind you have to do on your own. Off the cuff. Shooting from the lip. No notes, no outline, no prepared manuscript, nothing but your feeble mind to keep you going. You're not sure you'll make it through this part of Speech.

The teacher takes it easy on you at first. Your early topics are things like "What I Did on Christmas Vacation" or "My Favorite Baseball Team." It's rough being up there and trying to think and talk at the same time (something most of us don't like to do), but since the topics are nonthreatening you get through it. Then she assigns the real toughies: "What Newton's Law and Einstein's Theory of Relativity Have in Common with Sigmund Freud." They don't want a speech, they want a Ph.D. dissertation.

Survive it is all you want to do. Most of you will. If you do a good job, you'll find you're communicating better. You've lost some of your nasty speech habits, y'know? That's good, because the ability to communicate what you're thinking or feeling, wanting, or needing is important.

Speech class should also remind you that there's something else you need to speak out about—your faith. There will be lots of times when you'll have an opportunity to speak out about what a difference knowing Jesus makes in your life. Those will be important times—for you and the other person.

That's because you will be the only Jesus some people ever know. Think about it. Many of your friends probably don't go to church. Most of them, whether you realize it or not, know that you do. They watch you, to see what you're like. Are you just like them or is there some difference? Since they're not going to church and you are, you are showing them—by the life you live—what Jesus is like. They judge God by what they see and hear—or don't see and hear—from you. Is God kind, loving, compassionate, truthful, and bold? Or is God hateful, nasty, short-tempered, and mean? What are you saying about Jesus?

It's hard to use words to describe something as private as our faith. We know how we feel when God comes close to us. We don't want our friends to laugh off something that special, and us. But just like we had to get up the first time in Speech class and talk—no matter how scared we were—we need to talk about our faith to our friends. Like Speech class, after we do it once, it becomes easier and easier. All we're doing is sharing about one Friend with another. In this day of loneliness and isolation for so many of the people we know, what could be better?

Yes, Speech class—and talking about Jesus—can be terrifying. Palms may sweat, knees shake, and minds head for the bathroom door. But when it's over, it feels good to have communicated something of yourself to others. And maybe, just maybe, helped them on their way, too.

This course emphasizes the fundamentals of recordkeeping. Simulated business situations are presented. Apple IIE computers will be used to demonstrate automated accounting. Students will each utilize the computer when working through some business simulations. A vocational subject, it prepares students to become accountants, bookkeepers, clerks, and other business personnel. It is also recommended for persons going into business for themselves or anyone planning to major in business in college.

• • • •

Mr. Morgan: Our discussion today will center around accounting terminology. Who can tell me what *gross sales* means?
JoAnn: That's money derived from the sale of fake fly-in-an-icecube, plastic barf, . . .

• • • •

In Accounting you learn all kinds of things. One of them is how to use a spreadsheet. No, not a bedsheet, a *spreadsheet*. (I got confused at first, too). It's something that shows projected income and outgo and all sorts of other stuff. In Accounting you'll also encounter things like debits and credits, liabilities and assets. Put simply (which is the only way it should be put if I'm supposed to understand it), debits and liabilities can be seen as how much you owe and credits and assets are how much you are owed. But that's too simple to create any mystique, so the wonderful world of accounting was born. After taking Accounting you too will be able to use fancy "Accounting-ese" and amaze all your no-accounting friends.

Assets and liabilities are things we have in life, too. There they are called what we've got going for us and what we don't. Some of us have good looks. Some have zits. Some are smart. Others are not very. There are guys and girls who are graceful. There are kids who are klutzes. The amazing thing is that each one of us has a mixture of assets and liabilities. It may seem to us that we know people who have a lot more of one or the other than we do, but in life, like in accounting, these things usually balance out.

What is important, you see, is what's done with these assets and liabilities. There's even an accounting story in the Bible. Jesus tells about a boss who gave each of his three employees some money to manage while he was gone. Two of the three invested their money and when the boss returned gave him his money back—and more. This looked good on their ledger sheets. The third fellow, whose biggest liability was himself, hid the money in the ground, didn't do a thing with it, and when the boss came back, gave him just what he had been given—nothing more, nothing less. The boss was upset. He fired the man, figuring he was not too bright, maybe even downright dishonest. An accounting had been called for and he didn't pass the audit.

The reason he didn't was because he had something and didn't try to make more of it. He had potential, just like the other two, but was content to hide and hoard it. He didn't pull out the spreadsheet and see what he could do with what he had. Nothing ever came of it. In essence, it was wasted. It was a valuable resource squandered.

You have your assets, too. You may feel like you don't, but you do. You may need to take a little time, pull out the ledger book and look at yourself to find out what they are. If you're down on yourself, it may take longer. But the assets are there, regardless of what you think or how you feel. It's up to you what becomes of them—and you.

There are times when we all feel pretty worthless, especially when we compare ourselves with others around us. So we need to quit doing that. After all, we're unique, you and me. Think about it. We are ones of a kind. Originals. Custom-made. That in itself is an asset.

While you're sitting in Accounting, think of making up a spreadsheet on yourself. What's your future? What is in store for you? Begin by putting down your liabilities and your assets.

Then concentrate on your assets, forgetting all about the liabilities. Liabilities seem to take care of themselves, it's the assets that need attention. Then think of things you, and only you, can do. The way you walk. The way you talk. The way you care for some people that others may not be able to stand. Pretty soon you'll find the assets outweighing the liabilities.

God wants it that way. He wants you to be the best you can be. Not so that you can be egotistical. Rather so you will be realistic, recognize your strengths, and use them for His glory. God needs good people who are willing to look at their strengths and weaknesses—both of which He can use. God can be strong in our weakness and use our strengths to make the world a better place.

Pull out the ledger sheet and get to work. You've got a great future in accounting. You've got grand resources at your disposal—God and you.

This course is designed to introduce the student to the political system of the United States. This course will consider the U.S. Constitution, Bill of Rights, court procedures, the presidency, the legislative process, state and local governments, campaigns, and elections.

It will also compare our government with those of other nations. We will consider the governments of the countries of Europe, Latin America, and the communist nations, with some discussion of the nations of Asia, Africa, and the Middle East. This course is intended primarily for the serious student with an interest in world politics.

• • • •

Mrs. Phillips: Today we are going to talk about famous quotations from our nation's earliest days. What founding father said, "These are the times that try men's souls?"
Linda: That was mine—right after he looked at my last grade card.

• • • •

"Government of the people, by the people, and for the people." "Life, liberty, and the pursuit of happiness." If you haven't learned the above quotations by now, you will in Comparative Government. As the course description says, in this class you're going to learn all the details behind what makes our country work the way it does. You'll learn how old you have to be to be a congressman, senator, or president. You'll look at the Constitution and all its articles. (No, the Constitution is not a magazine; nor will it have any articles about the new punk-wave rhythm-and-blues rock group George and the Potomac Punks.) You might even organize political parties, hold mock elections, and run the school for one day. But don't count on the last part. The principal may let you sit in her office, but she'll run the place from the teachers' lounge every bit as well as the Godfather runs the Mafia from prison.

Even though you do learn a lot, sometimes it's hard to care very much about government. About the only time we're really interested in it is when some politician interrupts our favorite TV show to give a speech. Have you ever noticed how they never preempt something boring, like "Clam Digging on Cape Cod With Clyde Clark?" Nope, instead they break in during the best part of "Miami Vice Returns to Mayberry."

"You got 'em covered with your submachine gun, Crockett?"
"Sure do, Barney. You and Gomer sneak around—."
"We interrupt this program to bring you a live news conference from Senator Bill Backwater's office on a federal study on peanut butter sandwiches and their effect on. . . ."

Then the news conference will drag on until just after our folks have made us go to bed. It's enough to make you want to write your congressman.

Some of us have even been to Washington, D.C., on family vacations and remember things like the Smithsonian Institution, with all its exhibits, or seeing the White House and Capitol Hill or the Supreme Court. Just seeing them, though, doesn't mean we have any idea of how they work. Or how they affect us. And we should. Not just because that's what Comparative Government says we need to do if we're going to be good citizens. The reason we need to understand government is that we are the government. What happens to us is up to us. In Comparative Government we learn just how important our voice and vote and ideas are to where this country is going and what it is going to do. Comparative Government also raises another idea that needs to be dealt with: Who really governs our lives?

Comparative Government tells us that it's the folks in Washington, D.C., and other seats of government who do. To an extent, that is true. To another it's not. Those people may think they govern us; we know they don't. They may make the rules we live by as a nation, but in most of our everyday life, we, not they, decide how we are going to live. Our life is governed of the person, by the person, for the person.

Sometimes that goes okay. Other times it doesn't. We are

169

our own legislative, executive, and judicial systems all rolled into one. We like to think we are independent and self-sufficient. We don't need anyone to help us. Sometimes, though, living by our own laws gets us into places we'd just as soon not be. We've played dictator of our lives, and found out it wasn't as good as we had hoped. As hard to admit as it is, we just don't have enough information to always be able to pass the right legislation for living. We need to compare governments for our inner lives.

Comparative Government tells us about communism, fascism, dictatorships, and democracies. There is one that's left out. It's called a theocracy. That means God governs.

God wants to—but He wants to be more than a figurehead. God wants to be supreme ruler.

He doesn't want that because He's on an ego trip. Notice I didn't say God *needed* to govern, I said He *wanted* to. The reason God wants to do it all is that God is the only One who can do it right. If He leaves it up to us, we'll create domestic disasters all over the place.

The Christian life isn't a democracy. Not because God doesn't care about how you feel and what you want, but because He does. God cares very much. That's why He wants control. To make sure that only the very best in life comes your way. God knows you better than you know yourself. Therefore, He knows where to take your life to make it the best one possible. But to do that God has to be in charge. He won't force the issue, but that's what He wants. The Bible calls it the "abundant life."

While you're taking Comparative Government, you might want to do some comparisons of your own. What kind of government do you have in your life? Is it a dictatorship, ruled by you and you alone? Is it a democracy, with your friends' votes, as well as yours, governing your life? Does the government in charge really know what they are doing and have your best interests at heart? You may want to look at the Lord of the Universe and see about making Him Lord of your life. Is it time for a special election?

In this course students will learn to write simple INPUT/ OUTPUT programs, interactive programs which make use of loops, arrays, menus, and subroutines, and create and process data files. Students will also learn to manipulate graphics statements to create designs and games. Emphasis will be placed upon analyzing problems, designing flowcharts, and writing structured programs.

• • • •

Mr. Blacketeer: What seems to be the trouble with your Apple?
Paul: I don't know. Someone must have taken a byte out of it.

• • • •

Computers are an important part of modern life. They are everywhere. Every time you fire up the Firebird one is there, telling the car how to mix the fuel and the air for the best mileage. There's one in your microwave, telling it how long to defrost the pizza you want to feed your face. Computers control the temperatures in the school building and how fast or slow the elevators in downtown high-rises go. I'm writing on one now. Everywhere you go, chances are a computer is either helping you get there or helping you while you are there. That's nice, but sometimes scary. What happens when they break?

Computers do, you know. Break, that is. When they do they are just as dumb as a box of plastic, microchips, and wires can be. That's pretty dumb. Then the car won't start. The microwave turns the pizza into something that looks like Mount Saint Helens about to erupt. The air conditioner at school comes on and drops the room temperature to minus forty-five, when it's already minus forty-five outside. The elevator you tell to go to the second floor suddenly takes off like a rocket ship from Cape Canaveral. The next thing you know you've passed the 108th floor and you're heading for the moon! Yes, computers are great when they work right, and awful when they don't.

One thing every computer needs is someone to run it. That's why you see ads on television for schools that will turn you into a prime-time programmer, word processor, or computer technician.

Learn the exciting world of computers and make zillions of dollars a day. Enroll now in the Ace School of High Technology and Computer Stuff.

Computer people are needed because there are so many Apples, Apricots, and other fruits around.

I don't know about you, but I wasn't very excited about my first encounter with a computer. When I was a kid, computers had names like Brainiac and took up whole floors of downtown office buildings. They had lots of lights and dials and reminded me of something from "Chiller Theater" on Channel 10. Now they sit on desks, staring at you with their little cathode-ray eyes.

A cathode-ray tube (CRT) works the same as a television screen and all my life my mother told me not to sit too close to the TV set or the radioactivity it contained would turn me into a mutant. Now everyone wants to sit six inches away from a CRT—including my mom.

It also scared me to think a box that whirrs, typewriter keyboard without the carriage return, and miniature television screen is smarter than I am. (It's bad enough when living, breathing people are smarter, which most are, but it really hurts when you're dumber than a plastic box.)

What used to be accessible to only a few elite scientific minds is now available to everyone. They even teach little kids in grade school how to use the things. My son Ben, a twelve-year-old, has been using them longer than I have. He knows more about how they work and what they will and won't do than I do, too.

173

When you sign up for Computer Science, you'll be learning things that ten years ago they only taught in graduate school. You learn about bits and bytes, ROM and RAM, disk-operating systems, and all kinds of other things. Then there are words that you thought you knew the meaning of, but in computereze mean something completely different. *Loop* for instance. I always thought it was something you put in your shoelace before tying it. Sometimes it all seems to be coming so fast you wonder who's in charge, you or IBM?

Besides needing someone to operate them, there is one other thing common to all computers: They are only as smart as the stuff you put into them. They compute really fast, but they can't reason. If you entered a picture of a dog and called it a house, whenever that computer would see a dog it would call it a house. It can't help it. Once it's learned something you have to unlearn it for the machine. Otherwise it will continue to make the same stupid error over and over again. In other words, if your computer keeps giving you bad information it's because that's what you fed it in the first place. Computer users have long had a saying—"Garbage in, garbage out." What they mean is don't put bad stuff in and expect to get good stuff out. Don't expect the computer to think even simple thoughts for you. It's not that it won't—it can't.

So you don't ever have to feel threatened by one of these 512k wonders. It can only do what you tell it to do.

That's where we are different from a computer. We can think, we can reason. Unlike IBMs, Digitals, or Commodores, when we were put together we were constructed with the ability to think creatively. We can take raw data, think about it, and make our own decisions about courses of action. We aren't robots programmed to do one thing.

The Bible says God made us, for one thing, because He wanted some company. The angels were nice, but not enough. God had made them to worship Him and what choice did they have? Like computers, angels do what they are programmed to do. Then God made us. Humans. And gave us the choice of doing what we want. Love God or not. Obey God or not.

God doesn't make us do what He wants us to. It's up to us.

Remember that in computer class. You're not like the TRS-80 in front of you. It *has* to obey your commands. It has to do what you want. You, on the other hand, make your own choices for your life. Including what to do with God. That's up to you and you only. He wants your love and your life—but only if you want that too. Your programming is your own choice.

ENGLISH 12

Advanced-placement English, for seniors, English 12 combines serious literature study and advanced writing. Students successfully completing this course *may* qualify by test for college credit and advanced placement in college. The course will stress the development of the novel, the modern novel, and types of drama. Selections to be read include works of: Homer, Sophocles, Shakespeare, Austen, Tolstoy, Ibsen, Conrad, James, Shaw, Fitzgerald, Hemingway, Camus, and Hesse. The student will have the opportunity to work independently on reading and writing projects and on skill building (vocabulary, speed reading, grammar, etc.). This course also includes writing various kinds of themes and literary research papers.

• • • •

Ms. Record: Has everyone completed a biographical study of his or her favorite author?
Bruce: Well, I tried but I had a lot of problems. I couldn't find anything on him. When I asked the librarian she said she didn't have a listing on this person.
Ms. Record: Who is your favorite writer?
Bruce: It's someone named A. Nonymous.

• • • •

Just when you thought it was safe to go back to English, comes English 12. You've been taking English in one form or another since you were in kindergarten. You've gone from Richard Scarry to George Bernard Shaw. You've gamely gotten grammar and learned a lot of lit. You're beginning to feel like you may actually be literate. Now this. The course description alone sounds awfully scary, like something out of the current catalog from State U. What's worse is it's supposed to. If there is anything that schools don't want you to feel it is comfortable. "So you think you know something," they seem to say. "Well, we'll show you." And they do.

177

Take just a minute and look back at your first day in high school. Remember when you were a lowly freshman? There were all those feelings of being scared and intimidated just at being in high school? Now all that has changed. Finally, you're a senior. An upperclassperson. Top of the heap. You're one of the giants that little freshmen—even those taller than you— look up to. Even the smallest senior has so much more going for him or her than the finest freshman. Your mere presence intimidates. You have arrived.

But you can't stay on top forever. You've got nine months at most. As the above course description reminds you, graduation is ahead. You've been waiting for it for a long time. You've got your class ring, class key, and senior pictures. The prom is coming. Soon you'll be ordering caps and gowns. Then the big day will be here. You'll sit straight and proud as the alma mater is sung, speeches are given by the class valedictorian and others, and the principal begins handing out diplomas. You'll walk forward to get yours. Twelve long years are about to end. You'll shuffle out of the auditorium, clutching your diploma, your final act as a high school student. It'll be the last thing you do as a senior. Tomorrow you're a freshman again—in life.

After graduation comes college, vocational school, or a job. And once again, you'll be starting over. An underclassman. Bottom of the heap. It's not a very hot feeling. Instead of having arrived, you find high school graduation was just a rest area on life's freeway. The destination is still a long way off. There are lots of curves, potholes, fast straightaways, and detours on the road ahead. At seventeen or eighteen, with twelve years or so of school behind you, you're just beginning. There's a lot of life ahead of you. And a lot of changes.

There is one thing you do need to remember. No matter what changes in your life, there can be one thing that never changes. That's Jesus Christ. The Bible tells us He is the same yesterday, today, and forever. So, if He is part of your life today, you can count on Him being part of it forever. As long as you want to be friends with Him, He'll be there for you. The choice is yours. Many times we like to think we can handle

178

whatever life throws at us all by ourselves. So we do. Sometimes it goes okay; other times it doesn't. If we're honest we'll admit it would be nice to have something constant in the middle of all the changes.

We can have that if we let Jesus into our lives to stay. The Bible tells us there is a friend who sticks closer than a brother. It's great to have a real friend—one you can count on. It's good to know you have Someone who loves you and stands by you no matter if you goof everything up or do it right. It means no matter how bleak life may seem—and it does sometimes— you can go on because Jesus goes with you.

I hope this book has shown you that God cares about you and your life. Everything from the little to the big things, and everything in between. God can, and wants to, be involved in all of your life—including school. And after school. School, and life, if you'll let them, can teach you things about God. And you. And your life together.

Yes, English 12 and its complex course description remind you that you haven't got it all together yet. But you *are* on your way. Commencement—a beginning, not an end—is approaching quickly. You've got a Friend who lives inside you, who won't ever leave you. Keep in touch with that Friend and it won't be so bad to be starting all over at the bottom of the pile. Because with Jesus as your Friend, you're really not.